O Perfect Life of Love

Daily Lenten Meditations on J.S. Bach's *St. John Passion*

BRIAN J. HAMER

Emmanuel Press ✠ Fort Wayne, IN

Copyright © 2025 Brian J. Hamer
Published by Emmanuel Press
Fort Wayne, Indiana
www.emmanuelpress.us
emmanuelpress@gmail.com

Cover design: Meghan Schultz
The crucifix depicted on the cover hangs above the altar in Redeemer Lutheran Church, Fort Wayne, Indiana. The corpus was carved in Oberammergau, Germany; the cross was crafted by Pr. Mark Mumme.

English translations of the choruses, chorales, ariosos, and arias are by Francis Browne, reproduced with permission. www.bach-cantatas.com.

Unless otherwise noted, Scripture quotations are from The Holy Bible, English Standard Version®, copyright © 2001 by Crossway, a publishing ministry of Good News Publishers. All rights reserved.

Hymn texts and rites with the abbreviation *LSB* are from *Lutheran Service Book*, copyright © 2006 Concordia Publishing House. Used with permission. cph.org.

Excerpts from *The Small Catechism* from *Lutheran Service Book*, text © 1986 Concordia Publishing House. Used with permission. cph.org.

Hymn texts with the abbreviation *TLH* are from *The Lutheran Hymnal* © 1941 Concordia Publishing House. cph.org.

All rights reserved. No part of this book may be reproduced, stored in a retrieval system, or transmitted, in any form or by any means, electronic, mechanical, photocopying, recording, or otherwise, for financial profit without the prior written permission of Emmanuel Press.

ISBN 978-1-934328-29-3
Manufactured in the United States of America

"These are written so that you may believe that Jesus is the Christ, the Son of God."
John 20:31

Table of Contents

Before You Read and Listen v
Acknowledgements. vii
Ash Wednesday 1
The Week of Invocavit 11
The Week of Reminiscere 27
The Week of Oculi. 43
The Week of Laetare 61
The Week of Judica 77
Holy Week. 93
The Resurrection of Our Lord 108

BEFORE YOU READ AND LISTEN

It is probably just a coincidence that the New Bach Edition of the *St. John Passion* by J. S. Bach (1685–1750) divides Bach's masterwork into the same number of movements as there are days in Lent. This book of meditations places those forty movements of the *St. John Passion* as a literary and musical stencil over the forty weekdays *of* Lent—Ash Wednesday through Holy Saturday, excluding Sundays *in* Lent—to create a daily listening lectionary. I pray that this careful and deliberate approach to Bach's masterwork—forty movements in forty days—will assist you, the reader/listener, in your Lenten piety as you behold the life-giving cross, on which was hung the salvation of the world.

To use this volume, I suggest that you first select a non-Communion office from *Lutheran Service Book* (*LSB*) to frame your devotion. Bach first premiered the *St. John Passion* within the Order of Vespers (on Good Friday, April 7, 1724), but there are several options to choose from for use in the home, including Matins, Responsive Prayer II, or the Daily Prayers printed on page 294 in *LSB*.

Second, select a recording of the *St. John Passion* from a plethora of options. As I wrote these meditations, I was listening to the recording by the RIAS Kammerchor and the Akademie für Alte Musik Berlin (2016), which can be found on streaming services like Spotify and iTunes. If you wish to see the musicians, then consider a visually interesting rendition of the Passion by Netherlands Bach Society or a recording by Bach Collegium Japan (with subtitles) with conductor Masaaki Suzuki, both of which are available on YouTube. Hopefully your recording will label the movements 1–40 for ease of reference, but please be aware that some recordings follow a different numerical scheme.

Third, pray the non-Communion office every weekday during Lent, inserting the text of the *St. John Passion* (located at the top of each meditation) as one of the readings for the day. Ideally you will listen to a good German recording of the movement assigned to that day—the first movement for the first day of Lent, the second movement for the second day of

Lent, etc.—and follow along with the English. The English translation in the left-hand column is a combination of chorales and arias translated by Francis Browne and, where applicable, the words of Holy Scripture in the English Standard Version. Even if the German text in the right-hand column is not familiar to you, the meditations are designed to guide the non-German speaker to some key German words in the narrative and an appreciation of Bach's musical painting of the German text. However you approach the text and translation, I invite you to clear away all distractions, use your best sound equipment, and give Bach's lengthy work a fair hearing.

The meditation that follows the text of the Passion should be inserted into the daily office after the Scripture lesson as the meditation for the day. The prayer at the bottom of each meditation serves as a conclusion to the meditation or can be inserted into the prayers of the daily office. I encourage you to listen closely to the music, which serves as the living voice of the Gospel; to sing along, especially as you hear familiar hymn tunes; and finally, to pray repeatedly, revisiting these texts any time of year, but especially during holy Lententide.

It is the fervent prayer of the author that through these daily meditations God would "cast the bright beams of [His] light upon [His] Church that we, being enlightened by the doctrine of [His] blessed apostle and evangelist John, may come to the light of everlasting life" (Collect for St. John, Apostle and Evangelist).

Rev. Brian J. Hamer
Holy Cross Day 2024

Acknowledgements

Special thanks are due to my late father, Rev. John Hamer, whose faithful study of the Scriptures, especially his well-worn Hebrew Old Testament and Greek New Testament, first instilled in me a passion for the writings of St. John. I am grateful to Dr. Daniel Reuning, whose annual performances of the *St. John Passion* within the Lutheran Vespers kept this work alive for so many in the Lutheran Church—Missouri Synod. Dr. William Weinrich's monumental three-volume commentary on the Gospel of John, along with his thoroughly churchly and sacramental understanding of the text, continues to enrich (and challenge!) me and all who enjoy patristic studies and the occasional cigar. Dr. Burnell F. Eckardt Jr.'s book, *Every Day Will I Bless Thee: Meditations for the Daily Office*, shaped my theological and literary approach in writing, preaching Christ with great economy of words.

I am thankful to Rev. Jeffrey Horn and the faithful flock at Gloria Dei Lutheran in Escondido, California, for using this work as our parish Lenten devotional and for subsequently offering feedback. My wife, Jennifer, and our daughters, Kaitlyn and Emma, faithfully listened to the attendant music and the meditations throughout Lent 2023 and encouraged me to pursue publication. Christine Abernathy, John Bombaro, Tricia Ebner, Jane Hettrick, Bonnie Rex, Harold Senkbeil, and Christian Tiews all made helpful suggestions within their respective fields, as well as readers Jacob Benson, Peter Eckardt, and Stefan Gramenz. Their penchant for clarity and eye for detail have no doubt saved me from considerable embarrassment. Finally, I wish to thank Michael and Janet Frese at Emmanuel Press. I first approached Michael about this possibility at a casual conversation over breakfast early in 2023. I am grateful for his consideration and for presenting the manuscript to his wife and colleague, Janet, who handled the arduous yet rewarding task of cover-to-cover editing. Her subject matter expertise is exceeded only by her infinite patience, and for that I am grateful.

Ash Wednesday

The First Day of Lent

1. *Chorus*: Lord, our ruler

Lord, our ruler, whose glory	Herr, unser Herrscher, dessen Ruhm
Is magnificent everywhere!	In allen Landen herrlich ist!
Show us through your Passion,	Zeig uns durch deine Passion,
That you, the true Son of God,	Daß du, der wahre Gottessohn,
At all times,	Zu aller Zeit,
Even in the most lowly state,	Auch in der größten Niedrigkeit,
Are glorified!	Verherrlicht worden bist!

Traditionally, the reading of the Passion of our Lord from the Gospels begins with a brief introduction or exordium. The most ancient one for St. John is the following introduction, dating from the eighth century: "The Passion of our Lord Jesus Christ according to John," followed by a reading of St. John chapters 18 and 19.† The chorus printed above, "Lord, our ruler," replaces the ancient exordium and serves as a perfect introduction to Bach's *St. John Passion* and to our Lenten journey.

The opening chorus for full choir and orchestra echoes the first and last verses of Psalm 8, thereby serving as an antiphon or thematic statement for this chorus. Psalm 8, appropriately dedicated "To the Choirmaster," extols the Lord as the Creator, that is, as the One who has set His glory above the heavens and whose name is majestic through all the earth. The intervening Psalm verses, though not included in this chorus, describe the good gifts of creation (heaven and earth, moon and stars, etc.) and how God has given man, as the crown of creation, dominion over His handiwork. Indeed, His name is renowned throughout the heavens and the earth, for He created all things for His glory and for your enjoyment.

---

† Paul Hillier, *Arvo Pärt Oxford Studies of Composers* (Oxford and New York: Oxford University Press, 1997), 123.

The second portion of the chorus ("Show us through your Passion," etc.) shifts the focus from the Father's work of creation to the Son's redemption of creation. God's glory is above the firmament, but He does not leave His glory there. The introduction to John's Gospel (1:1–14) proclaims the good news that the Word of the Father became flesh and dwelt among us. Similarly this chorus preaches the good news that the very Son of God, begotten of the Father from eternity, was glorified precisely in His humiliation. Christ's Passion in His glorification and His being "lifted up" (John 3:14) is His exaltation and the full revelation of God. He opted for mockery over praise and scourging instead of adoration. But as the lessons and customs for Lent and Holy Week demonstrate every year, God's highest glory is to redeem your flesh by giving His own flesh into suffering and death (John 12:27, 32–33), thereby restoring the splendor of creation.

Hear the message of man's rejection of God and God's redemption of man in this opening chorus! The dissonance in the oboes—evident from the opening measure—creates a sense of tension that is fitting for the rejection of the Creator. The pulsing in the lower registers of the chamber orchestra sounds like a heart frantically reacting to the awful price of sin, as sure as placing ashes on your forehead today is the fullest expression of the Law. But the chorus sings richest and purest Gospel, proclaiming the good news that the Word incarnate came from heaven, redeemed you through the humiliation of the cross, and returned to heaven. And you too shall pass through death to the joys of eternal life with God.

Christ, my God—who by death did trample death,
who, being One of the Holy Trinity, is glorified
with the Father and the Holy Spirit—save me!
Amen.

Thursday after Ash Wednesday
The Second Day of Lent

2. Evangelist, Jesus, Crowd: Jesus went out with his disciples

Jesus went out with his disciples across the brook Kidron, where there was a garden, which he and his disciples entered. Now Judas, who betrayed him, also knew the place, for Jesus often met there with his disciples. So Judas, having procured a band of soldiers and some officers from the chief priests and the Pharisees, went there with lanterns and torches and weapons. Then Jesus, knowing all that would happen to him, came forward and said to them, "Whom do you seek?" They answered him, "Jesus of Nazareth." Jesus said to them, "I am he." Judas, who betrayed him, was standing with them. When Jesus said to them, "I am he," they drew back and fell to the ground. So he asked them again, "Whom do you seek?" And they said, "Jesus of Nazareth." Jesus answered, "I told you that I am he. So, if you seek me, let these men go."

Jesus ging mit seinen Jüngern über den Bach Kidron, da war ein Garten, darein ging Jesus und seine Jünger. Judas aber, der ihn verriet, wusste den Ort auch, denn Jesus versammlete sich oft daselbst mit seinen Jüngern. Da nun Judas zu sich hatte genommen die Schar und der Hohenpriester und Pharisäer Diener, kommt er dahin mit Fackeln, Lampen und mit Waffen. Als nun Jesus wusste alles, was ihm begegnen sollte, ging er hinaus und sprach zu ihnen: Wen suchet ihr? Sie antworteten ihm: Jesum von Nazareth. Jesus spricht zu ihnen: Ich bin's. Judas aber, der ihn verriet, stund auch bei ihnen. Als nun Jesus zu ihnen sprach: Ich bin's, wichen sie zurücke und fielen zu Boden. Da fragete er sie abermal: Wen suchet ihr? Sie aber sprachen: Jesum von Nazareth. Jesus antwortete: Ich hab's euch gesagt, daß ich's sei, suchet ihr denn mich, so lasset diese gehen!

After the short introductory movement, the narrative shifts to the longer sections of the Passion, often identified by geographic location. St. John begins in the garden, a place where the biblical narrative traditionally reveals the strength of the Law and the consolation of the Gospel, from the first paradisial union in Genesis 1–2 to its restoration in the new creation in Revelation 21–22.

The brook Kidron is more than a passing detail along the way. The idea of crossing over in the biblical narrative is indicative of key redemptive events: Israel crossing through the Red Sea on dry ground; Israel entering the promised land through the river Jordan; David fleeing from Jerusalem after his betrayal by Absalom; and Jesus, Israel reduced to One, standing in the Jordan to be anointed into His own death. At this point in the Passion, then, Jesus was crossing His own Rubicon (with profound significance: it was His last crossing before His passion). Also significant is the garden. The other Evangelists call it Gethsemane, but John omits the name, perhaps to encourage you to think of the Garden of Eden and its restoration in Christ.

As the first garden in the Bible was invaded by the serpent, so this garden was tainted by the spiritual sons of Satan, as depicted by Bach's sudden shift to minor chords at the mention of Judas. Jesus had just told Judas, "What you are going to do, do quickly" (John 13:27), and Judas obeyed straightaway, fleeing into both visceral and spiritual darkness. Then Jesus immediately said, "Now is the Son of Man glorified" (John 13:31), proclaiming yet again the good news that His glorification begins not in His signs of power or in any earthly trophies, but in the most infamous kiss of betrayal in human history.

The music of this movement thus far is a basic musical recitation of the narrative, sung by a single tenor with minimal instrumental accompaniment. Jesus' question, "Whom do you seek?" sung by the bass, leads to the first crowd or *turba* chorus, which Bach uses whenever groups of people are speaking. The sense of urgency to arrest Jesus is evident as all the voices, with full instrumental support, declaim with fervent vigor, "Jesus! Jesus! Jesus of Nazareth!"

Jesus' reply, "I am he," is theologically laden. Jesus said that the revelation of "I am" would occur when the betrayer lifted his heel against Him (John 13:18), and so it is fulfilled. Moreover, Jesus uttered several "I am" statements in John's Gospel, but the most pertinent one in this context is certainly the following claim, which deeply offended the religious establishment: "Before Abraham was, I am" (John 8:58). Here Jesus takes the Hebrew name, "I AM WHO I AM" (Exod. 3:14) as a spark of His divinity pierces the night of betrayal and reveals Him to be Yahweh made flesh. His command to "let these men go" shows that He willingly goes into captivity to release you from slavery and to grant you baptismal sonship with God the Father.

Vindicate me, O God, and defend my cause against an ungodly people. (Ps. 43:1)
Amen.

Friday after Ash Wednesday
The Third Day of Lent

3. *Chorale*: O great love

O great love,	O große Lieb,
O love without any limits,	O Lieb ohn' alle Maße,
That has brought you	Die dich gebracht
Along this martyr's way!	Auf diese Marterstraße!
I lived with the world	Ich lebte mit der Welt
In pleasure and delight,	In Lust und Freuden,
And you must suffer.	Und du musst leiden.

This movement brings you to the first chorale or German hymn in the *St. John Passion*. The principal text of Bach's choral masterwork is chapters 18 and 19 of the Gospel according to St. John. But along the way, an anonymous scholar known generically as the librettist—working closely with the composer—inserted several chorale stanzas and a few other poetic texts to serve as sermonic commentary on the Passion narrative.

This particular chorale stanza is drawn from the hymn, "O Dearest Jesus, What Law Hast Thou Broken" (*LSB* 439:7). The author of the text, Johann Heermann (1585–1647), was a poet and pastor in Silesia during a devastating time of plague, war, and illness. The area where Heermann lived was plundered four times by Roman Catholic forces of the Thirty Years' War. He lost all of his possessions several times and at one point was forced into hiding for nearly four months. One contemporary rightly described him as "the Silesian Job." Heermann's understanding of life under the cross as expressed in his hymns ranks him among the finest German hymn writers, along with Martin Luther (1483–1546) and Paul Gerhardt (1607–1676).

The melody hails from Johann Crüger (1598–1662), who served in the most prestigious church music position in Germany in his day, Kantor of St. Nicholas Church in Berlin. During the last five years of his tenure there, he worked with Paul Gerhardt, who is widely regarded as an eloquent Lutheran hymnwriter. The harmonization is of course by J. S. Bach, who never wrote a hymn text or melody but rather harmonized, used, and promoted pre-existent texts and tunes, with rich harmonies and various musical settings for voices and instruments. As it were, three men—all named Johann—joined forces across the years on this first chorale stanza in the *Johannes-Passion*.

This hymn stanza is sung between the arrest in the garden and the Evangelist's proclamation that Jesus' arrest fulfills His words that He would not lose any of His sheep (John 10:28). How fitting to pause and proclaim the "great love...without any limits," the unconditional love of God that finds its highest expression in Jesus' Passion. See how Jesus' sacrificial love is the antithesis to your sin, which keeps you curved in on yourself and your heart set on earthly treasures. In contrast to Judas' pursuit of a few paltry coins, Jesus procured heavenly treasure for you and thereby became your eternal treasure.

Jesus was led along the martyr's way. His suffering is the price paid for your life of pleasure and delight. There is a chromatic descent at this point in the chorale, signifying this path of torment, with the choir sighing in anguish. This is then contrasted briefly with the melismatic figure in the alto part on "delight" (*Freuden*), only to return to the sound of suffering with the dimished chords in the final phrase "and you must suffer" (*und du musst leiden*)—but ending on a hopeful G-Major chord. And you, O believer, turn from earthly pleasures and delight this Lent, forsaking your life in this world (John 12:25), that you may receive Christ by faith and adore His cross.

And when, dear Lord, before Thy throne in heaven
To me the crown of joy at last is given,
Where sweetest hymns Thy saints forever raise Thee,
I, too, shall praise Thee. (LSB 439.15)
Amen.

Saturday after Ash Wednesday
The Fourth Day of Lent

4. Evangelist, Jesus: This was to fulfill the word

This was to fulfill the word that he had spoken: "Of those whom you gave me I have lost not one." Then Simon Peter, having a sword, drew it and struck the high priest's servant and cut off his right ear. (The servant's name was Malchus.) So Jesus said to Peter, "Put your sword into its sheath; shall I not drink the cup that the Father has given me?"	Auf daß das Wort erfüllet würde, welches er sagte: Ich habe der keine verloren, die du mir gegeben hast. Da hatte Simon Petrus ein Schwert und zog es aus und schlug nach des Hohenpriesters Knecht und hieb ihm sein recht Ohr ab; und der Knecht hieß Malchus. Da sprach Jesus zu Petro: Stecke dein Schwert in die Scheide! Soll ich den Kelch nicht trinken, den mir mein Vater gegeben hat?

Of those whom you gave me I have lost not one" (John 18:9). With these words, Jesus fulfilled the promise that He made in His high priestly prayer when He said, "While I was with [the disciples], I kept them in your name, which you have given me. I have guarded them, and not one of them has been lost except the son of destruction, that the Scripture might be fulfilled" (John 17:12).

See how Christ, your great High Priest in human flesh, drinks the ultimate cup of sacrifice to save you. The two most unique tasks of the high priest of the Old Testament were eating the bread of the Presence (Exod. 25:30) and sprinkling blood on the Day of Atonement (Lev. 16). Recall that the priests prepared the bread of the Presence, carefully placed it in God's sanctuary, and ate it as a sacred meal. The message of the sacred bread was clear: God was present through eating.

The other task reserved strictly for the priest was the liturgy of the annual Day of Atonement, when the high priest entered the Holy of Holies and sprinkled the blood of the atonement on the mercy seat. As the hymn puts it, "Where the paschal blood is poured, death's dread angel sheathes the sword" (*LSB* 633.3).

Bread and blood come together in John's portrait of Christ. Jesus multiplied the loaves in the feeding of the five thousand (John 6:1–15) and gathered twelve baskets of leftovers (John 6:12–13), foreshadowing the bread of the Last Supper and the ingathering of God's people (John 6:14). Thus, the One who brings the bread of this life and who is the Bread of heaven shall not lose one of His faithful disciples. And the same One who provides these gifts from the Father will enter the Holy of Holies of the Father's presence in His death to win the forgiveness that now flows from the chalice to your very lips.

The music becomes more dramatic and intense to depict Peter's feeble attempt to rescue Jesus. Poor Peter. This is reminiscent of a scene in J. R. R. Tolkien's *The Lord of the Rings*, which contrasts the culture of life (immortal elves, magical bread, etc.) with the culture of death (a ring of absolute power, goblins and orcs, etc.). When Gandalf the Wizard leads the nine members of the fellowship out of the mines of Moria, they are confronted by a Balrog, the demon of the ancient world. To his companions, armed with traditional armor, Gandalf speaks profound words: "Swords are of no use here!" Gandalf must face the ancient demon alone while the other eight members of the fellowship flee for their lives.

So sheathe your sword, Peter! Bach's ascending melody illustrates the drawing and lifting of the sword, while the descending melody on "and cut off his right ear" (*und hieb ihm sein recht Ohr ab*) depicts Peter's sword striking Malchus. The physical sword had a place in God's Old Testament army, the military branch of the only true theocracy in world history (Num. 31). But at this key moment in the Passion, swords of steel are of no value. The only sword that remains is the sword of the Spirit (Eph. 6:17), the Word of God.

See how your incarnate Priest and the scriptural sword work diligently for you and your salvation. Christ, your great high Priest, wields the two-edged sword of His Word, bringing you to repentance and preaching forgiveness to your ears. And because Jesus insisted on drinking the cup of suffering, ordering Peter's sword to be sheathed, you may drink the cup of life in His blessed Sacrament.

Soul of Christ, hallow me; body of Christ, save me; blood of Christ, refresh me. Amen.

The Week of Invocavit

*"He shall call upon me,
and I will answer Him."*

Psalm 91:15

Monday of Invocavit
The Fifth Day of Lent

5. *Chorale*: Your will be done, Lord God

Your will be done, Lord God, both	Dein Will gescheh, Herr Gott, zugleich
On earth as in heaven.	Auf Erden wie im Himmelreich.
Grant us patience in time of suffering,	Gib uns Geduld in Leidenszeit,
Obedience in love and sorrow;	Gehorsam sein in Lieb und Leid;
Restrain and guide our flesh and blood	Wehr und steur allem Fleisch und Blut,
That acts against your will!	Das wider deinen Willen tut!

You might recognize this melody from Martin Luther's hymn based on the Lord's Prayer, "Our Father, Who from Heaven Above" (*LSB* 766). Like many of his hymns, Martin Luther here built on ancient treasures, such as Psalms, catechetical texts, and liturgical texts. In this case, he adapted the Lord's Prayer into a nine-stanza hymn: one for the introduction to the Lord's Prayer, one for each of the seven petitions, and one for the doxological conclusion.

The words "your will" (*dein Will…deinen Willen*) serve as textual bookends to this stanza and therefore as the primary theme. The concept of God's will, however, has not fared well in modern American evangelicalism. Books aplenty—appropriately classified as self-help on the bookshelf—encourage you to seek God's will regarding everything from how to become a "better you" to how to find the best parking spot at the mall. In this line of thinking God is like the game master in an escape room, offering clues on how to predict His next move, solve the puzzles of daily living, and eventually escape the quandary of knowing and doing God's will in spiritual and temporal matters. Yet those who try to probe the hidden counsel of God are seemingly unaware that God our heavenly Father executes His will in spiritual matters without our prayer. Moreover, He leaves many temporal matters to sanctified common sense, that is, to our Christian freedom to make daily decisions within the boundaries set by the Ten Commandments.

So what is this hymn stanza proclaiming at this point in the narrative, just after Jesus' arrest and Peter's ill-fated attempt to protect his Savior? Martin Luther explains the Third Petition in Section III of his *Small Catechism*:

How is God's will done?

> God's will is done when He breaks and hinders every evil plan and purpose of the devil, the world, and our sinful nature, which do not want us to hallow God's name or let His kingdom come; and when He strengthens and keeps us firm in His Word and faith until we die. This is His good and gracious will.

Under the Law, the unholy triad—the devil, the world, and your own sinful flesh—would have Jesus avoid the cup of suffering for your sins and encourage Peter to fight a losing battle with his sword. These three great enemies of God's people likewise tempt you to ask every day why bad things happen to good people, instead of beholding the life-giving cross and asking why *good* things happen to *bad* people because of one truly good Man.

Even without your prayer, God's gracious will always prevails in your life. The Father's will prevailed before His throne when Christ willingly went to the cross of suffering. He gives you strength when you are weak and "patience in time of suffering." How fitting that the melody meanders up and down, with ascending lines to depict your prayer and descending lines to depict God's gifts coming down from heaven to fulfill His will to keep you "firm in His Word and faith until [you] die."

> *When life's brief course on earth is run*
> *And I this world am leaving,*
> *Grant me to say: "Thy will be done,"*
> *By faith to Thee still cleaving. (TLH 517.4)*
> *Amen.*

Tuesday of Invocavit
The Sixth Day of Lent

6. *Evangelist*: So the band of soldiers and their captain

So the band of soldiers and their captain and the officers of the Jews arrested Jesus and bound him. First they led him to Annas, for he was the father-in-law of Caiaphas, who was high priest that year. It was Caiaphas who had advised the Jews that it would be expedient that one man should die for the people.	Die Schar aber und der Oberhauptmann und die Diener der Jüden nahmen Jesum und bunden ihn und führeten ihn aufs erste zu Hannas, der war Kaiphas Schwäher, welcher des Jahres Hoherpriester war. Es war aber Kaiphas, der den Jüden riet, es wäre gut, daß ein Mensch würde umbracht für das Volk.

A coalition of Roman and Temple guardsmen led Jesus from the garden back to Jerusalem. We then read that they led Jesus first to Annas, "the father-in-law of Caiaphas, who was high priest that year" (John 18:13). Why did they lead him first to Annas? And what was the relationship between Annas and Caiaphas, as well as the relationship between Judaism and the Roman empire?

Here is what we know for sure: Annas was a former high priest, father of five high priests, and the influential father-in-law of the current high priest, Caiaphas. The curiosity of historians ancient and modern is compounded by the removal of Annas from his office by the Romans about fifteen years before Jesus' arrest. Under normal circumstances high priests were appointed annually (John 11:49; 18:13). The simultaneous involvement of Annas and Caiaphas suggests that the Romans meddled in the appointment process. Moreover, Judaism had a high regard for patriarchy from Abraham to the present day, so it would not be surprising for them to consult the elder Annas before moving on to Caiaphas.

Even more important than these historical details, however, is how this scene benefits you and bears fruit in your life: "one man should die for the people" (John 18:14). You probably want to say, "Amen, Amen!"—but in agreement with a purpose that Caiaphas never imagined. As an opponent of Jesus, he spoke these words in an earlier exchange with some priests and Pharisees (John 11:46–50). They asked Caiaphas about Jesus' miracles and how to respond to them, saying, "If we let [Jesus] go on like this, everyone will believe in him, and the Romans will come and take away both our place and our nation" (John 11:48). Caiaphas was encouraging a sacrifice of political expediency, rather than the all-atoning sacrifice. But again, his words are correct: one man will die for the sins of the people.

One is reminded here of the breastplate worn by the high priest of the Old Testament. Recall that the breastplate had twelve stones, one for each tribe of Israel (Exod. 28:6–14). The twelve-stoned breastplate indicated that the Aaronic priest conducted the word and "sacraments" of the Old Testament for the people. The Old Testament liturgy was from God, by the priests, and for the people. In other words, it was from God, mediated by the priests, and for the salvation of God's people. Especially on the annual Day of Atonement (Lev. 16), one man embodied every man as he entered the Holy of Holies and sprinkled the blood of the atonement for Israel. The author of Hebrews says that Christ, your great high priest, "entered once for all into the holy places, not by means of the blood of goats and calves but by means of his own blood, thus securing an eternal redemption" (Heb. 9:12).

Listen for a large melodic leap up to the word "man" (*Mensch*), highlighting the importance of the one Christ. Also notice the dramatic slowing down on the verb "die" (*umbracht*), encouraging you to linger at the cross for a while this Lent.

What Thou, my Lord, hast suffered
Was all for sinners' gain;
Mine, mine was the transgression,
But Thine the deadly pain. (LSB 450.3)
Amen.

Wednesday of Invocavit

The Seventh Day of Lent

7. Aria (Alto): From the bonds of my sins

From the bonds of my sins	Von den Stricken meiner Sünden
To set me free,	Mich zu entbinden,
My Savior is bound.	Wird mein Heil gebunden.
From all infections of vice	Mich von allen Lasterbeulen
To heal me completely,	Völlig zu heilen,
He gives himself to be wounded.	Läßt er sich verwunden.

This is the first aria in the *St. John Passion*. The Italian term aria (i.e. air or melody) signifies an extended solo that allows you, the hearer of the sacred music, to pause and meditate on the text, the first section often repeated for further meditation.

This poem builds on the language of Jesus' arrest. Picture Jesus (to use a modern context) in handcuffs, leg irons, and an orange jumpsuit that says "RJDC" on the back—Roman and Jewish Department of Corrections. He is being led like a leashed animal to the ultimate kangaroo trial to be denied by a close follower, undergo untold suffering, and suffer the death of an insurrectionist. What does this mean for you and for your salvation?

Recall Jesus' parabolic saying about the strong man: "Or how can someone enter a strong man's house and plunder his goods, unless he first binds the strong man? Then indeed he may plunder his house" (Matt. 12:29). That is to say, "How can I, the strongest Man, enter Satan's worldly domain and plunder his goods unless I first bind Satan by removing the sting of death? Only then may I plunder his goods."

The poetic text of this aria echoes the same themes as this short parable of Jesus. On your own, you are bound to "the bonds of [your] sins" and "infections of vice." You inherited Adam's sin and cannot free yourself from the snares of your sin any more than you can raise yourself from the dead. Musically, did you hear how the two oboes play the same music, with one following slightly behind the other? This is a musical form known as a canon (a fixed law or standard), in which the second voice is bound to imitate the first, note for note. This reminds us of God's Law, which commands you to be holy as He is holy and to follow in His steps. But you soon discover that you are, in the words of one of Luther's hymns, "fast bound in Satan's chains" (*TLH* 387.2).

Jesus, led away like a common criminal, willingly goes to His suffering to untie the snares of sin that once bound you to eternal death. Consider the following "voice of Christ" text from one of Luther's hymns: "The foe shall shed My precious blood, Me of My life bereaving" and "All this I suffer for thy good" (*TLH* 387.8). And what are the goods in Jesus' parabolic saying about the strong man? What does Jesus come to claim? You, dearly beloved! Yes, you are the goods or treasure created by God, stolen by Satan in the fall into sin, and now reclaimed by Christ in His Passion.

The phrases beginning with "from" in this aria are examples of a type of prayer known as deprecation, that is, a petition to avert sin and danger by prayer. So you, otherwise fast bound in Satan's kingdom, pray for release from sin and death and to be kept safe in the nail-pierced hands of Jesus.

From all sin, from all error, from all evil;
from the cords of my sin, from the infection of wickedness,
and from everlasting death: Good Lord, deliver me.
Amen.

Thursday of Invocavit
The Eighth Day of Lent

8. *Evangelist*: Simon Peter followed Jesus

Simon Peter followed Jesus, and so did another disciple.

Simon Petrus aber folgete Jesu nach und ein ander Jünger.

This is one of the shortest movements of the *St. John Passion* and of Bach's entire repertoire. There are two possible reasons for this tantalizing brevity. The librettist who compiled the text pauses at key points in the narrative to insert poetic texts (arias and chorales) to interpret the biblical text. The idea of following Jesus is a fitting time to pause and explore the cost of discipleship, which occurs in the next movement.

Another possible reason is the old adage that "less is more." The movement is so brief—only half of a Bible verse, a few seconds in most recordings—that it tends to highlight itself, for every word is pregnant with meaning. Whatever the reason for the brevity, let us pause mid-week during Invocavit and briefly consider the discipleship of Peter and John and how they, after some slips along their own roads of following Jesus, were faithful unto death.

Peter followed Jesus and, as you know, denied Jesus as impetuously as he had vowed never to leave Jesus. Recall from John 13 that Jesus said to Peter, "Where I am going you cannot follow me now, but you will follow afterward" (v. 36)—a veiled prophecy of Peter's own martyrdom. Looking ahead in the biblical narrative, Peter's threefold denial was offset, so to speak, by Jesus' threefold charge to feed the flock (21:15–19), which Peter did faithfully as a leader in the early church and as the most prominent preacher in the first half of the Acts of the Apostles. The hymn "By All Your Saints in Warfare" includes a stanza which references Peter and gives words of thanksgiving and admonition to all the sheep in God's little flock:

> Praise for Your great apostle
>   So eager and so bold,
> Thrice falling, yet repentant,
>   Thrice charged to feed Your fold.
> Lord, make Your pastors faithful
>   To guard Your flock from harm,
> And hold them when they waver
>   With Your almighty arm. (*LSB* 517.10)

In contrast to Peter, John neither denied nor deserted Jesus. Together with the mother of our Lord, he stood faithfully at the foot of the cross. Jesus even gave her into John's keeping; according to church tradition, Mary lived with him until her death. After Pentecost, John lived for a time in Jerusalem and eventually settled in Ephesus. It was there that he wrote his three letters, the Book of Revelation, and the Gospel which bears his name and became the foundational text for Bach's *St. John Passion*. History suggests that he was the only Apostle not to be martyred, although he suffered during his exile in Patmos, as the hymn relates:

> For Your belov'd disciple
>   Exiled to Patmos' shore,
> And for his faithful record
>   We praise You evermore.
> Praise for the mystic vision
>   Through him to us revealed;
> May we, in patience waiting,
>   With Your elect be sealed. (*LSB* 517.8)

> *For these, passed on before us,*
> *We offer praises due*
> *And, walking in their footsteps,*
> *Would live our lives for You. (LSB 517.4)*
> *Amen.*

Friday of Invocavit
The Ninth Day of Lent

9. *Aria (Soprano)*: I follow you likewise with joyful steps

I follow you likewise	Ich folge dir gleichfalls
With joyful steps	Mit freudigen Schritten
And do not leave you,	Und lasse dich nicht,
My life, my light.	Mein Leben, mein Licht.
Bring me on my way	Befördre den Lauf
And do not cease	Und höre nicht auf,
To pull, push, and urge me on.	Selbst an mir zu ziehen,
	zu schieben, zu bitten.

Yesterday's meditation discussed the history of Peter and John following Jesus after His arrest. Today's devotional text addresses the theology of discipleship, that is, what it means for you to follow Jesus.

This text applies the concept of discipleship or following to you, the hearer of the narrative. The first half of the text paraphrases Peter's bold assertion to follow Jesus, come what may, but places the text in your mouth as your own confession of faith. Christ is your life and your light, so following Him keeps you on the narrow way that leads to eternal life. The flutes begin the melody while the soprano echoes it, a simple yet profound portrait of following Christ, your Head.

And yet, this path is not without its stumbling blocks and even perilous threats. In this movement you pray for Jesus to carry you along the path, to guide you without ceasing, and to draw, push, and implore you on the path of life. The music takes a brief but dramatic turn to paint this part of the text—"pull, push, and urge"—as if depicting how Christ the Good Shepherd uses the crook of the Law to call you to repentance and set you back on the road to eternal life when you stray.

One is reminded here of Dietrich Bonhoeffer (1906–1945), the Lutheran pastor, theologian, and spy who was executed in World War II for his role in the Valkyrie plot to kill Hitler. His book, *The Cost of Discipleship* (originally titled *Nachfolge*, or "following") is among the works on the Christian faith which is worth not just tasting or chewing, but digesting again and again. Writing during a time of severe persecution for the Church, Bonhoeffer famously wrote of discipleship, "When Christ calls a man, He bids him come and die."† That is to say, you, O disciple, must die to your sinful self through repentance, bear your cross of suffering for the sake of the Gospel, and continually follow Jesus through death to eternal life. Bonhoeffer wrote his words in the 1930s; they were fulfilled in greatest measure for him when he was hung from the gallows in a German death camp just after the Second Sunday of Easter in 1945.

There is one more aspect to the music that is striking to me. Did you notice how joyful it sounds? Two buoyant flutes play a joyful, dance-like melody in 3/8 meter (think of a waltz) and in a major key. Meanwhile, the soprano—considered to be a symbol of human prayer in Bach's day—floats effortlessly above the modest cadre of instruments. This music proclaims in clear and joyous tones that your journey, though beset with danger, is taken "with joyful steps" (*mit freudigen Schritten*), for "you have died, and your life is hidden with Christ in God" (Col. 3:3). Moreover, "If we have died with him, we will also live with him" (2 Tim. 2:11).

> *Blessed Jesus, Son of God:*
> *Guide me that I never may*
> *From Your fold or pastures stray,*
> *But with zeal and joy exceeding*
> *Follow where Your steps are leading. (LSB 692.1)*
> *Amen.*

---

† Dietrich Bonhoeffer, *The Cost of Discipleship* (NY, NY: Touchstone, 1995), trans. John W. Doberstein, 89.

Saturday of Invocavit
The Tenth Day of Lent

10. *Evangelist, Servant Girl, Peter, Jesus, Servant*: Since that disciple was known

Since that disciple was known to the high priest, he entered with Jesus into the courtyard of the high priest, but Peter stood outside at the door. So the other disciple, who was known to the high priest, went out and spoke to the servant girl who kept watch at the door, and brought Peter in. The servant girl at the door said to Peter, "You also are not one of this man's disciples, are you?" He said, "I am not." Now the servants and officers had made a charcoal fire, because it was cold, and they were standing and warming themselves. Peter also was with them, standing and warming himself. The high priest then questioned Jesus about his disciples and his teaching. Jesus answered him, "I have spoken openly to the world. I have always taught in synagogues and in the temple, where all Jews come together. I have said nothing in secret. Why do you ask me? Ask those who have heard me what I said to them; they know what I said."	Derselbige Jünger war dem Hohenpriester bekannt und ging mit Jesu hinein in des Hohenpriesters Palast. Petrus aber stund draußen für der Tür. Da ging der andere Jünger, der dem Hohenpriester bekannt war, hinaus und redete mit der Türhüterin und führete Petrum hinein. Da sprach die Magd, die Türhüterin, zu Petro: Bist du nicht dieses Menschen Jünger einer? Er sprach: Ich bin's nicht. Es stunden aber die Knechte und Diener und hatten ein Kohlfeu'r gemacht (denn es war kalt) und wärmeten sich. Petrus aber stund bei ihnen und wärmete sich. Aber der Hohenpriester fragte Jesum um seine Jünger und um seine Lehre. Jesus antwortete ihm: Ich habe frei, öffentlich geredet für der Welt. Ich habe allezeit gelehret in der Schule und in dem Tempel, da alle Jüden zusammenkommen, und habe nichts im Verborgnen geredt. Was fragest du mich darum? Frage die darum, die gehöret haben, was ich zu ihnen geredet habe! Siehe, dieselbigen wissen, was ich gesaget habe.

When he had said these things, one of the officers standing by struck Jesus with his hand, saying, "Is that how you answer the high priest?" Jesus answered him, "If what I said is wrong, bear witness about the wrong; but if what I said is right, why do you strike me?"	Als er aber solches redete, gab der Diener einer, die dabeistunden, Jesu einen Backenstreich und sprach: Solltest du dem Hohenpriester also antworten? Jesus aber antwortete: Hab ich übel geredt, so beweise es, daß es böse sei, hab ich aber recht geredt, was schlägest du mich?

This scene is a literary tug of war between Peter's denial and Jesus' trial before the high priest. This split-screen approach serves to reveal the strength of the Law and the consolation of the Gospel.

Peter thought he was faithfully fulfilling his promise to follow Jesus along the narrow road to eternal life, but he was about to take the broad road to destruction in one of the most notorious denials in church history. Did you notice how the music becomes very dramatic at the mention of the servant girl (*die Magd*)? Here is a turning point for Peter: This anonymous young lady posed no intrinsic threat to him, but her preference for extroversion, combined with an evening of messianic fervor and hatred for the truth, escalated Peter's risk. Peter's denial is abrupt and direct, both in text and in music: "I am not!" Peter continued warming himself by the fire, an apparently small detail which will grow in importance after Jesus is risen from the dead (John 21:9).

Meanwhile, Jesus stood before the high priest to be tried for blasphemy. Nicodemus said that Jewish law permitted a hearing for the accused (John 7:51), so the faux high priest asked the true High Priest about His teaching and that of His followers. See how Truth Himself speaks one divine truth: He indeed taught openly before the world in the synagogue, the temple, and in the open air. The music then changes abruptly—"When he had said these things"—to depict the servant striking Jesus, fulfilling the word spoken through Isaiah, "I hid not my face from disgrace and spitting" (Isa. 50:6).

And what about the charcoal fire? The only other charcoal fire mentioned in the entire New Testament occurs at Jesus' resurrection appearance in John 21. After catching 153 fish at the Lord's command, the disciples hurried to meet Jesus on the shore, where there was "a charcoal fire in place" (John 21:9). Jesus then charged Peter to feed His sheep (John 21:15–19). At the first charcoal fire, Peter crumbled under pressure and was brought to the depths of remorse and repentance. At the second fire, however, Peter affirmed his love for the Lord, received the charge to feed the flock that Jesus purchased with His own blood, and did so with his own cross in the foreground: "[W]hen you are old, you will stretch out your hands, and another will dress you and carry you where you do not want to go. (This he said to show by what kind of death he was to glorify God.)" (John 21:18–19). Peter embraced the charge to feed the flock, encouraging his hearers to know that "when the chief Shepherd appears, you will receive the unfading crown of glory" (1 Pet. 5:4).

Similarly, you, O sinner, have often denied your baptismal identity by your sin and have grieved over your sin in repentance. But Christ comes to you in His means of grace, gives you faithful pastors to tend to you as His own lamb, and grants you to confess His saving name.

Let your priests be clothed with righteousness,
and let your saints shout for joy. (Ps. 132:9)
Amen.

The Week of Reminiscere

*"Remember, O Lord, Thy tender mercies
and Thy lovingkindnesses."*

Psalm 25:6

Monday of Reminiscere

The Eleventh Day of Lent

11. *Chorale*: Who has struck you in this way

Who has struck you in this way,	Wer hat dich so geschlagen,
My Savior, and with torments	Mein Heil, und dich mit Plagen
Treated you so badly?	So übel zugericht?
You are indeed not a sinner	Du bist ja nicht ein Sünder
As we and our children are;	Wie wir und uns're Kinder;
Of wrongdoing you know nothing.	Von Missetaten weißt du nicht.
I, I and my sins,	Ich, ich und meine Sünden,
That are as many as grains	Die sich wie Körnlein finden
Of sand by the sea,	Des Sandes an dem Meer,
Have provoked for you	Die haben dir erreget
The misery that has struck you	Das Elend, das dich schläget,
And the host of troubles and torment.	Und das betrübte Marterheer.

These chorale stanzas come from Paul Gerhardt's hymn, "Upon the Cross Extended" (*LSB* 453:3, 4). Gerhardt knew suffering quite well. In addition to losing his wife, multiple children, and his post as pastor, he also lived through the Thirty Years' War, the battle between the Roman Catholic and Protestant armies which decimated much of Europe from 1618 to 1648. This hymn was written at the end of this protracted war, a most fitting time to contemplate the parallels between Christ's suffering and ours.

The first stanza allows you, the hearer of the Passion, to enter into dialogue with the innocent Jesus as He stands before the high priest: "Who has struck you in this way," etc. Here you ponder why the innocent One — "You are indeed not a sinner"—is treated as the guilty One and rushed to trial, to conviction, and ultimately to the death of an insurrectionist: "Christ also suffered once for sins, the righteous for the unrighteous, that he might bring us to God" (1 Pet. 3:18).

The second stanza answers the questions posed in the first. As you can imagine, much ink has been spilt through the centuries to answer the question, Who killed Jesus? On a human level, He was betrayed by Judas, denied by Peter, tried by unbelievers, sentenced by Pilate, and crucified by Roman soldiers. God the Father, of course, ultimately sent His Son to die for you, and the Son willingly gave Himself into death. But the emphasis here is the relationship between your sin and Jesus' death: "I, I and my sins…provoked…the host of troubles and torment."

See how you, O sinner, have been wounded by the sin you inherited from Adam. You have not just inherited Adam's sin; you have participated in Adam's sin, even from conception, by your fault, by your own fault, by your own most grievous fault. But the good news is this: "For while we were still weak, at the right time Christ died for the ungodly" (Rom. 5:6). Thus are you saved by the wounds of the new and greater Adam (Rom. 5:12–21), for His affliction has cast your sins, though countless as grains of sand, into the sea to save you from sin and eternal death.

Your cross I place before me;
Its saving pow'r restore me,
Sustain me in the test.
It will, when life is ending,
Be guiding and attending
My way to Your eternal rest. (LSB 453.7)
Amen.

Tuesday of Reminiscere
The Twelfth Day of Lent

12. *Evangelist, Crowd, Peter, Servant*: Annas then sent him

Annas then sent him bound to Caiaphas the high priest. Now Simon Peter was standing and warming himself. So they said to him, "You also are not one of his disciples, are you?" He denied it and said, "I am not." One of the servants of the high priest, a relative of the man whose ear Peter had cut off, asked, "Did I not see you in the garden with him?" Peter again denied it, and at once a rooster crowed. And Peter remembered the saying of Jesus and went out and wept bitterly.

Und Hannas sandte ihn gebunden zu dem Hohenpriester Kaiphas. Simon Petrus stund und wärmete sich, da sprachen sie zu ihm: Bist du nicht seiner Jünger einer? Er leugnete aber und sprach: Ich bin's nicht. Spricht des Hohenpriesters Knecht einer, ein Gefreundter des, dem Petrus das Ohr abgehauen hatte: Sahe ich dich nicht im Garten bei ihm? Da verleugnete Petrus abermal, und alsobald krähete der Hahn. Da gedachte Petrus an die Worte Jesu und ging hinaus und weinete bitterlich.

The contrast between Jesus and Peter is stark: Jesus stands up to His questioners and denies nothing; Peter cowers before his questioners and denies everything. But the end of this story—recorded by all four Evangelists—is programmatic for your baptismal life of repentance and restoration.

His face probably illumined by the charcoal fire, Peter's identity as a follower of Jesus quickly spread to the crowds, leading to one of Bach's *turba* or "crowd" choruses: "You also are not one of his disciples?" Hear how Bach masterfully paints a picture of the unbelievers gathering around Peter. The musical theme is repeated in rapid succession, producing a vivid musical portrait of a highly-charged atmosphere of interrogation and unrest.

"[A]t once a rooster crowed." After three reliable witnesses identified Peter, his heart surely broke with agony as he went out and wept bitterly. Listen for a jagged and extended melodic line on the words "wept bitterly" (*weinete bitterlich*), one of the longest and most sorrowful lines in the Passion.

What does this mean for you and for your salvation? Consider St. Paul's words to young Timothy: "If we have died with him, we will also live with him; if we endure, we will also reign with him; if we deny him, he also will deny us; if we are faithless, he remains faithful—for he cannot deny himself" (2 Tim. 2:11–13).

Behold the grace of God: outrageous, lopsided, and grossly unfair to the rational human mind. We have all heard it in our daily lives, but it is rarely true: "You owe me!" Our natural mindset is captive to the opinion of the Law: emotionally detached, ruthlessly calculating, and artificially entitled to anything from earthly mammon to eternal life itself. But if God's gifts are rights instead of privileges, then they are no longer the Gospel. So do not presume on God's grace or claim His gifts by right, for under the Law He owes you nothing but wrath and displeasure.

But you have been baptized. You have died to sin through repentance. You will live with Him eternally. You have endured with Him, so you will also be a co-regent with Him in glory. Conversely, if you deny Him to the point of losing your faith and dying in unbelief, then you will forfeit your eternal salvation.

And yet, the most striking feature of Paul's saying is certainly the final clause, with its unexpected grammatical and theological twist: even if you deny Him (like Peter in his threefold denial), God remains faithful, for He cannot disown Himself. Behold the great comfort for you this Lent, especially as you mourn your most prominent denials of Christ. God is faithful, so there is no sin that you have committed that is not covered by Jesus' blood. As He did for Peter, God lifts you up in Christ, restores you to baptismal sonship, and gives you the peace that passes all understanding.

O Lord, grant that I may endure everything for the sake of the elect,
that they too may obtain the salvation which is in Christ Jesus.
Amen.

WEDNESDAY OF REMINISCERE
The Thirteenth Day of Lent

13. *Aria (Tenor)*: Ah, my soul

Ah, my soul,	Ach, mein Sinn,
Where will you at last go,	Wo willt du endlich hin,
Where shall I find relief?	Wo soll ich mich erquicken?
Should I stay here, or should I wish	Bleib ich hier, oder wünsch ich mir
That hills and mountains were at my back?	Berg und Hügel auf den Rücken?
In the world there is no help,	Bei der Welt ist gar kein Rat,
And in my heart are the pains	Und im Herzen stehn die Schmerzen
Of my wrongdoing,	Meiner Missetat,
Since the servant	Weil der Knecht
Has denied the Lord.	Den Herrn verleugnet hat.

For this aria, J.S. Bach uses an adaptation of the first stanza of a poem by Christian Weise (1642–1708), "Der weinende Petrus," or "The Weeping Peter." Here the librettist draws upon the first of five stanzas that capture Peter's remorse and applies it to your life by asking, Where do you go for help in your hour of deepest need?

The first half of the aria for tenor expresses Peter's deep remorse and utter despair over denying his Lord. Can Peter go to Jesus? Alas, He is on trial and being questioned by the high priest. Should Peter find a father confessor among the many priests in Jerusalem? The entire priestly establishment is no help, for they are long on ceremonial regulations but devoid of the forgiveness that Peter so desperately needs.

Again, where does Peter turn? The reference to "hills and mountains" in the first stanza of this aria recalls the sorrowful women on the road to the cross. To them Jesus said, "Daughters of Jerusalem, do not weep for me, but weep for yourselves and for your children. For behold, the days are coming when they will say, Blessed are the barren and the wombs that never bore and the breasts that never nursed!" (Luke 23:28–29). Should Peter join them to weep in sympathy for his Lord?

The second half of the aria dismisses what one might call "imaginary forgiveness." In the world—yes, in the secular world, hell-bent on its own pleasures, autonomy, and false gods—there is no counsel whatsoever. This is most certainly true, for our help must come from above, not from the fallen world. The world encourages you to search your heart to find anything from personal contentment to spiritual gifts. Even worse is the oxymoron "self-forgiveness." There is no such thing. All detours around the cross leave you in Peter's deep remorse and, apart from the word of absolution, in eternal despair.

Before answering the question of where you go for help, first consider the form and presentation of this aria. The musical form or style is a dance in triple meter, known as the *sarabande*, which was intended for royalty at court. The triple meter is especially fitting for Peter, who denied Jesus three times and who will not find forgiveness apart from the crucified King. Moreover, you may have noticed that the aria's ending is rather abrupt, offering a quick transition into the next movement. Perhaps this is Bach's way of encouraging you to move beyond Peter's lament and go to the divine tribunal where your loving King grants the word of absolution to you.

So back to the original question for Peter and for every disciple of Jesus: Where do you go to get full and free forgiveness? The answer will gradually unfold as you continue through the *St. John Passion*, looking outside your sinful heart to the cross of Christ, dwelling at the cross awhile to consider the One who suffered for your sin to bring rich and abundant life to you.

O Lord, thank you for the prophetic word made sure.
Grant that I may hear the word of the cross in penitent faith
until the day dawns and the morning star rises in my heart.
Amen.

Thursday of Reminiscere
The Fourteenth Day of Lent

14. *Chorale*: Peter, who does not think back

Peter, who does not think back at all,	Petrus, der nicht denkt zurück,
Denies his God,	Seinen Gott verneinet,
But then at a look of reproach	Der doch auf ein' ernsten Blick
Weeps bitterly.	Bitterlichen weinet.
Jesus, look at me also	Jesu, blicke mich auch an,
When I am reluctant to repent;	Wenn ich nicht will büßen;
When I have done evil,	Wenn ich Böses hab getan,
Stir up my conscience!	Rühre mein Gewissen!

Peter's lament transitions quickly into this chorale. As with every chorale or German hymn in the *St. John Passion*, the text is carefully chosen. This stanza here is from Paul Stockmann's (1603–1636) hymn, "Jesus' Suffering, Pain and Death," which was integral to Good Friday services in seventeenth- and eighteenth-century German Lutheran worship. This chorale is a congregational reflection on the Gospel narrative and encourages you, the hearer, to pause and consider Jesus' person and work through a familiar musical form.

"Peter, who does not think back" has two possible meanings. It can indicate that Peter denied Jesus without thinking, that is, that he was out of his mind. Or the phrase can mean that Peter did not remember Jesus' prediction of Peter's betrayal (John 13:38). The phrase "denies his God" refers to a brief scene in Luke's Passion where Jesus turned and looked at Peter at the moment of denial (Luke 22:61). The ornamentation (i.e., the moving parts) on "weeps bitterly" (*bitterlichen weinet*) recalls the lengthy bout of tears on these same words in Movement 12.

In this hymn stanza, then, Peter serves as a pattern for the congregation, inviting all the faithful to meditate on their own sinfulness. Recall that every sin denies your baptismal identity. Let us sharpen the sword of the Law and expand even further into some questions based on the

Second Commandment: Is the Lord's Word evident in your daily speech and conduct, or do you curse, speak carelessly, or misuse God's name? Do you keep all the vows that you have made in the Lord's name, such as confirmation, marriage, or legal vows? Are you diligent and sincere in your prayers, or have you been lazy, bored, or distracted? Do you trust that the Lord God will answer them according to His good and gracious will? See how you have denied God—and repent!

The second half of the chorale stanza takes the form of a prayer as the believer asks Jesus to glance upon him in grace and favor. As every parent will attest, raising children is a daily exercise in the application of the Law and the Gospel. When a child disobeys God and other authorities, for example, discipline often begins with a stern look, followed by an explanation of the Ten Commandments and a call to repentance. Upon the child's confession, the Law yields to the Gospel as parents embrace their own flesh and blood in grace and favor. This reflects God's way of dealing with His people, from turning His face away from them when they are impenitent to making His face shine upon them when the Christian conscience is stirred to lay one's sins at the foot of the cross in repentance and faith.

At this point in the Good Friday afternoon Vespers in Bach's Leipzig, the first half of the *St. John Passion* was finished. The musicians paused while the pastor preached on the subject of Jesus' burial from Isaiah 53 or Psalm 22. How comforting to know that Jesus buried your sins in His grave and left them there, so that He was entombed while you are set free.

To raise those who fall and to strengthen those that stand;
and to comfort and help the weak hearted and the distressed:
we implore You to hear us, O Lord.
Amen.

Friday of Reminiscere

The Fifteenth Day of Lent

15. *Chorale*: Christ, who makes us blessed

Christ, who makes us blessed	Christus, der uns selig macht,
And has done no wrong,	Kein Bös' hat begangen,
Was for us in the night	Der ward für uns in der Nacht
Seized like a thief,	Als ein Dieb gefangen,
Led before godless people	Geführt für gottlose Leut
And falsely accused,	Und fälschlich verklaget,
Derided, mocked, and spat upon,	Verlacht, verhöhnt und verspeit,
As the Scripture says.	Wie denn die Schrift saget.

Following the sermon on Jesus' burial, Bach resumed his place at the harpsichord, the musicians retuned their instruments, and the *St. John Passion* recommenced with a chorale. These words, along with a stately yet solemn tune in the minor mode, set the stage for Jesus' trial before Pilate.

The text is the first stanza of a hymn by Michael Weisse (ca. 1488–1534), who converted to Protestantism one year after Luther's *Ninety-Five Theses* and wrote first-generation vernacular hymns, that is, German hymns for German folk within Luther's lifetime.

The German text of "Christ, who makes us blessed" was influenced by a Latin hymn which was part of a cycle of texts that coordinated the eight daily prayer hours with the events of Jesus' Passion. The stanza for midnight Matins reminds the worshiper of what happened to Christ at that same hour:

> Circled by His enemies, by His own forsaken,
> Christ the Lord at Matin hour for our sakes was taken:
> Very Wisdom, Very Light, Monarch long expected,
> In the garden by the Jews bound, reviled, rejected.

Building on this text, the first part of "Christ, who makes us blessed" describes His innocence and His arrest, but the heart of the chorale text is certainly its description of all that Jesus endured before Pilate. The verbs in this chorale text coordinate closely with the verbs in Jesus' second Passion prediction in St. Luke: "[The Son of Man] will be *delivered* over to the Gentiles and will be *mocked* and *shamefully treated* and *spit upon*. And after *flogging* him, they will *kill* him" (Luke 18:32–33, emphasis added). Listen closely to the final phrases of the chorale for a dissonant melodic line of consecutive chromatic steps, which depict the deviousness of those who mocked the Christ.

See how He did it all for you! He was delivered to the Gentiles that you might be presented to God the Father. He was mocked by men, that you might be blessed by God; insulted, that you might be encouraged in your faith; spit upon, that you would be smiled upon; flogged, that you might escape the punishment that you have deserved. He was killed that you might have life and have it abundantly. And He rose from the dead that you might never die eternally.

We adore Thee, O Christ, and we bless Thee,
who by Thy holy cross hast redeemed the world;
Thou who hast suffered death for us, O Lord, have mercy on us.
Amen.

Saturday of Reminiscere
The Sixteenth Day of Lent

16. *Evangelist, Pilate, Crowd, Jesus*: Then they led Jesus

Then they led Jesus from the house of Caiaphas to the governor's headquarters. It was early morning. They themselves did not enter the governor's headquarters, so that they would not be defiled, but could eat the Passover. So Pilate went outside to them and said, "What accusation do you bring against this man?" They answered him, "If this man were not doing evil, we would not have delivered him over to you." Pilate said to them, "Take him yourselves and judge him by your own law." The Jews said to him, "It is not lawful for us to put anyone to death." This was to fulfill the word that Jesus had spoken to show by what kind of death he was going to die. So Pilate entered his headquarters again and called Jesus and said to him, "Are you the King of the Jews?" Jesus answered, "Do you say this of your own accord, or did others say it to you about me?" Pilate answered, "Am I a Jew? Your own nation and the chief priests have delivered you over to me.

Da führeten sie Jesum von Kaiphas vor das Richthaus, und es war frühe. Und sie gingen nicht in das Richthaus, auf daß sie nicht unrein würden, sondern Ostern essen möchten. Da ging Pilatus zu ihnen heraus und sprach: Was bringet ihr für Klage wider diesen Menschen? Sie antworteten und sprachen zu ihm: Wäre dieser nicht ein Übeltäter, wir hätten dir ihn nicht überantwortet. Da sprach Pilatus zu ihnen: So nehmet ihr ihn hin und richtet ihn nach eurem Gesetze! Da sprachen die Jüden zu ihm: Wir dürfen niemand töten. Auf daß erfüllet würde das Wort Jesu, welches er sagte, da er deutete, welches Todes er sterben würde. Da ging Pilatus wieder hinein in das Richthaus und rief Jesu und sprach zu ihm: Bist du der Jüden König? Jesus antwortete: Redest du das von dir selbst, oder haben's dir andere von mir gesagte? Pilatus antwortete: Bin ich ein Jüde? Dein Volk und die Hohenpriester haben dich mir überantwortet;

What have you done?" Jesus answered, "My kingdom is not of this world. If my kingdom were of this world, my servants would have been fighting, that I might not be delivered over to the Jews. But my kingdom is not from the world."	was hast du getan? Jesus antwortete: Mein Reich ist nicht von dieser Welt; wäre mein Reich von dieser Welt, meine Diener würden darob kämpfen, daß ich den Jüden nicht überantwortet würde; aber nun ist mein Reich nicht von dannen.

How cold and calloused is the impenitent heart! As you see here, the heart curved in on itself and set against Christ will gladly deliver the innocent One to be crucified but zealously safeguard the man-made laws of purity by not entering the governor's headquarters. So it went for several generations of Jews, who added their own regulations to God's Law and therefore lost track of the Gospel itself. Listen for the first choral section—"If this man were not doing evil" (*Wäre dieser nicht ein Übeltäter*), etc.—wherein Bach conveys the unbelievers talking (and the musicians singing) simultaneously, as they rage against the anointed One.

After Pilate tried to return Jesus to the Jews, they revealed their true intentions: "It is not lawful for us to put anyone to death." The entanglement of Mosaic Law with later Jewish additions complicates the scene a bit, but the essence of the narrative is clear: the unbelieving Sanhedrin, along with their troops and servants, demanded Jesus' death and nothing less. Listen for the emphasis on the word related to putting to death (*töten*), with several rising and falling small steps in all four voices, bringing the reality of the cross into view and fulfilling Jesus' words that He will be lifted up on the tree of the cross (John 12:32–33). The rightful king will be rejected by His people in His own city.

Thus two kingdoms—one of this world, one from above; one that is temporal, another that is eternal—collide as Pilate questions Jesus. Pilate stands in continuity, for instance, with others in John's Gospel who secularized Jesus' lordship by hearing it in earthly terms. After the feeding of the 5,000, the unbelievers tried to force him to be their bread king (John 6:15). At His entry into Jerusalem, the crowds hailed him as "the King of Israel" (John 12:13), but their enthusiasm was premature, their minds set on a worldly kingdom rather than a kingdom under the cross.

The two kingdoms also converge in Jesus' dialogue with Pilate. In Jesus' final statement, "My kingdom is not from the world," the bass voice ascends to the traditional tenor range on the final occurrence of the word "kingdom" (*Reich*), suggesting that His kingdom is from above. Like Pilate, you are a member of the temporal realm, wherein you honor the emperor (1 Pet. 2:17). But a higher priority than any worldly realm is your baptismal membership in God's Kingdom, where cross precedes crown.

O King of the nations, the ruler longed for, the cornerstone uniting all people:
Come and save us all, whom You formed out of clay.
Amen.

THE WEEK OF OCULI

"Mine eyes are ever toward the Lord."

Psalm 25:15

Monday of Oculi

The Seventeenth Day of Lent

17. *Chorale*: Ah, great king

Ah, great king,	Ach großer König,
Great in all ages,	Groß zu allen Zeiten,
How can I make my faithfulness	Wie kann ich gnugsam
In any way adequate?	Diese Treu ausbreiten?
No human heart	Keins Menschen Herze
Can conceive	Mag indes ausdenken,
What gift is fit to offer you.	Was dir zu schenken.
My mind cannot imagine	Ich kann's mit meinen Sinnen nicht erreichen,
What can be compared to your mercy.	Womit doch dein Erbarmen zu vergleichen.
How then can I match your loving deeds	Wie kann ich dir denn deine Liebestaten
By anything I do?	Im Werk erstatten?

Building thematically on Jesus' declaration that His kingdom is "not of this world" (John 18:36), here the librettist once again inserts stanzas from Johann Heermann's hymn, "O Dearest Jesus, What Law Hast Thou Broken" (*LSB* 439: 8, 9). In spite of His appearance, Jesus is in fact the eternal King on the eternal throne, fulfiller of the Davidic line and holder of the scepter of eternal power, world without end. See the tension between the eternal nature of Christ's kingship in the cosmic order (1 Tim. 1:17; Rev. 19:16) and His temporal suffering. Where the religious authorities saw Jesus as an evil doer, Bach's congregation and all the faithful are invited to behold Him as the eternal King of all creation.

The question posed in the first stanza above reminds us that we are beggars before the King of kings. What do you have to offer the crucified King? Nothing—or at least nothing that Jesus needs. While it is tempting to sympathize with Jesus as you trace His road to the cross, the simple fact is that Jesus did not endure His Passion to conjure your sympathy. Rather, in Christ you "do not have a high priest who is unable to sympathize with [your] weaknesses, but one who in every respect has been tempted as [you] are, yet without sin" (Heb. 4:15).

The second stanza in this movement reminds you of the limitations of your human wisdom, for the mysteries that you ponder this Lent are about faith, not human reason. Listen carefully in the lower registers of the orchestra for something called a "walking bass," that is, a series of shorter notes that support the upper three voices yet sound rather labored. This music depicts human reason laboring in vain to give a gift to the crucified King. But the text, forsaking all human reason, draws you to God's unconditional mercy, which is meant to be received, not explained; believed, not rationalized.

Delving further into the hymn, Heermann directs you above all human reason to the true fruits and benefits of Jesus' Passion. How do you ponder Jesus' Passion this Lent? Heermann suggests forsaking "earth's vain joys" (st. 12); taking up one's cross ("no cross shall daunt me," st. 13); and relying firmly on God's grace ("Thou wilt accept my gift in Thy great meekness," st. 14). These final stanzas roughly correspond to Jesus' three-fold command for you to deny your sinful self, take up your cross of suffering, and to follow Jesus through death to life eternal (Mark 8:34).

And when, dear Lord, before Thy throne in heaven
To me the crown of joy at last is given,
Where sweetest hymns Thy saints forever raise Thee,
I, too, shall praise Thee. (LSB 439.15)
Amen.

Tuesday of Oculi

The Eighteenth Day of Lent

18. *Evangelist, Pilate, Jesus*: Then Pilate said to him

Then Pilate said to him, "So you are a king?" Jesus answered, "You say that I am a king. For this purpose I was born and for this purpose I have come into the world—to bear witness to the truth. Everyone who is of the truth listens to my voice." Pilate said to him, "What is truth?" After he had said this, he went back outside to the Jews and told them, "I find no guilt in him. But you have a custom that I should release one man for you at the Passover. So do you want me to release to you the King of the Jews?" They cried out again, "Not this man, but Barabbas!" Now Barabbas was a robber. Then Pilate took Jesus and scourged him.

Da sprach Pilatus zu ihm: So bist du dennoch ein König? Jesus antwortete: Du sagst's, ich bin ein König. Ich bin dazu geboren und in die Welt kommen, daß ich die Wahrheit zeugen soll. Wer aus der Wahrheit ist, der höret meine Stimme. Spricht Pilatus zu ihm: Was ist Wahrheit? Und da er das gesaget, ging er wieder hinaus zu den Jüden und spricht zu ihnen: Ich finde keine Schuld an ihm. Ihr habt aber eine Gewohnheit, daß ich euch einen losgebe; wollt ihr nun, daß ich euch der Jüden König losgebe? Da schrieen sie wieder allesamt und sprachen: Nicht diesen, sondern Barrabam! Barrabas aber war ein Mörder. Da nahm Pilatus Jesum und geißelte ihn.

Pilate's question—eternal and probing, ontological and philosophical—was more significant than he ever knew: What is truth, King Jesus? What say you? Jesus once said to the Jews who believed in Him, "You will know the truth, and the truth will set you free" (John 8:32). This one divine truth is inextricably linked to Jesus' incarnation and crucifixion, which are the bookends of Jesus' ministry in John's Gospel. Jesus' reply to Pilate echoes this truth of John 8 that He came to this world as Truth Incarnate, that all who hear His voice might hear the truth and be set free from sin and eternal death. His claim to one divine truth is the reason that the unbelievers reject Him, for "now you seek to kill me, a man who has told you the truth that I heard from God" (John 8:40). All other so-called truths lead to eternal death.

One Truth made flesh stands in contrast to the modern idea of tribal truth. A once-popular daytime talk show host, for instance, asked thousands of her guests to tell their story with these words: "Tell me your truth." You see the problem here, don't you? Her presupposition, a hallmark of postmodernism, was that there are many truths all created equal. Some call it tribal truth, that is, a truth for each like-minded group. Thus conservatives have their truth and progressives have theirs. Other nations, even those that legally beat and grievously injure wives and children, are considered equal to nations where the natural family is at the center of life. Or consider how many parents have spent hundreds of thousands of dollars to send their children to universities where they learn that there is no such thing as absolute truth, a "truth" of which the secularized university is absolutely certain!

In contrast to all false teaching and faux truth, Bach highlights Jesus' identity as one incarnate Truth in unique ways. The word "king" (*König*) is pitched in the upper register in Pilate's question, "So you are a king?" This same word, however, is echoed back to Pilate in the two lowest notes that Jesus sings in the entire Passion: "You say I am a king." As Jesus' subsequent words on coming into this world proclaim, He is the incarnate King, who took the lowest place on this earth that you might know the truth and share in the King's portion of life and salvation. Moreover, all references to the truth (*Wahrheit*) are set in the "trumpet key" of D Major, a key of glory (think, for instance, of the music to "Awake, My Heart, with Gladness"), most fitting for you as you hear and believe in one Incarnate Truth and receive life in His name (John 10:27–28).

This scene ends with the flogging of Jesus, a theme which will shape the next two movements. For now, consider the elaborate melisma (two or more notes on one syllable of text) on the word "scourged" (*geisselte*). There are a remarkable fifty-three notes on this jagged melisma. Do you remember the significance of the number fifty-three in the Old Testament? It is closely associated with Isaiah's Suffering Servant passage (Isa. 52:13–53:12, i.e., usually referred to in theological shorthand as Isaiah 53), which was an optional text for the Good Friday sermon in Leipzig. Do the fifty-three notes, spread over an expansive range of an octave and a half, depict the good news that Truth Himself fulfills the prophecy of Isaiah 53 for you and for your salvation?

> *O Lord, sanctify me in Your truth. Your word is truth.*
> *Amen.*

WEDNESDAY OF OCULI

The Nineteenth Day of Lent

19. *Arioso (Bass)*: Consider, my soul

Consider, my soul,	Betrachte, meine Seel,
With anxious delight,	Mit ängstlichem Vergnügen,
With bitter pleasure	Mit bittrer Lust
And half-oppressed heart,	Und halb beklemmtem Herzen,
That your highest good	Dein höchstes Gut
Depends on Jesus' sorrow,	In Jesu Schmerzen,
How for you, from the thorns that pierce him,	Wie dir auf Dornen, so ihn stechen,
Heavenly flowers blossom!	Die Himmelsschlüsselblumen blühn!
You can gather so much sweet fruit	Du kannst viel süße Frucht
From his wormwood;	Von seiner Wermut brechen,
Therefore look unceasingly towards him!	Drum sieh ohn Unterlaß auf ihn!

As you consider the history and fruits of Jesus' Passion, how do you react? The sinful flesh might be tempted to take a detour around the cross and avoid all talk of suffering and any mention of blood. But then Easter will seem rather hollow, for what value is the risen Christ without the suffering Christ? At the other extreme, some Christians through the centuries have focused solely on re-enacting the Passion, in some extreme cases actually inflicting bodily suffering on oneself or one's neighbor to try to feel exactly what Jesus endured.

This text draws you to the unresolved paradox and ongoing tension that is inherent to the suffering Christ. The first part of the aria describes your Lenten piety with several nearly synonymous terms—"anxious delight," "bitter pleasure," and perhaps the best description of repentance: "half-oppressed heart." This is your posture at the foot of the cross. Your pleasure is bitter because your sin killed Jesus. And yet your repentant heart, full of confident faith in Jesus, finds "that your highest good depends on Jesus' sorrow," for He did it all to save you from your sin and to bring you to Him. The overall unsettled nature of this contemplative aria suggests the bitter joy and penitent heart that is yours as you behold the life-giving cross, on which was hung your salvation.

But what, precisely, is the fruit of Jesus' suffering for you? The delightful tongue-twister *Himmelsschluesselblumen*, literally "keys-of-heaven flowers," bloom at the foot of the cross. The hearers in Bach's day would think of the cowslips flower, sometimes called "keys of Heaven" because of their resemblance to small keys. The idea of flowering or budding is an image of the third day of creation, of life, and of resurrection (Gen. 1:9–13). Moreover, St. John uses the key motif in Revelation to depict Jesus' power to open heaven to you, the believer, and conversely to close heaven to the impenitent (Rev. 1:18, 3:7). The keys-of-heaven flowers, then, depicted by the blossoming of rich harmonies, proclaim the good news that Jesus is the key and door to paradise—Eden restored—where you have new life with God.

The tenor repeats the call to look upon Him "without ceasing" for emphasis, followed by an extended cadence. This is a profound musical portrait of living your entire life under the cross as you behold, believe, and receive Him who is your life and salvation.

Faithful cross, true sign of triumph,
Be for all the noblest tree;
None in foliage, none in blossom,
None in fruit thine equal be;
Symbol of the world's redemption,
For the weight that hung on thee! (LSB 454.4)
Amen.

Thursday of Oculi
The Twentieth Day of Lent

20. *Aria (Tenor)*: Ponder well how his back, bloodstained

Ponder well how his back,	Erwäge, wie sein blutgefärbte Rücken
Bloodstained all over,	In allen Stücken
Is like the sky	Dem Himmel gleiche geht,
Where, after the deluge	Daran, nachdem die Wasserwogen
From our flood of sins has abated,	Von unsrer Sündflut sich verzogen,
The most beautiful rainbow appears	Der allerschönste Regenbogen
As a sign of God's mercy!	Als Gottes Gnadenzeichen steht!

Yesterday's sacred text was set to a short aria or arioso, a musical form that usually introduces a full-length aria. Today you encounter what yesterday's text prepared you for, that is, the rainbow on Jesus' blood-tinged back.

The music is intimate, meditative, and introspective. Long, drawn-out vowels give the impression of active and extensive contemplation, coupled with musical waves in the vocal line. Key words such as "ponder" (*erwäge*), "bloodstained" (*blutgefärbter*), and "the sky" (*dem Himmel*) are essentially torn up by rapid notes in the instrumental parts, a reminder of the brutal scourges of the Roman soldiers. The text, then, invites you to consider the heavenly fruits of Jesus' suffering, while the instruments remind you of the history of Jesus' Passion.

The second part of the text (starting at the word "where") draws upon imagery from the flood narrative in Genesis 6–8, especially God's promise, symbolized by the rainbow, that He would never again destroy the world by a flood. Recall that Noah and his family repopulated the earth after the flood waters receded. The anonymous poet uses this imagery for the forgiveness of sins. As the waters around Noah's ark once receded and made way for life, so the waves of your sin have receded in Jesus' Passion. His blood paid the price for your sin. He washed away your sins in the font of Holy Baptism, draping you in the baptismal robe that makes you right with God. Through Baptism you stand before God as if you were the very Son of God Himself, holy and righteous in His sight.

Consider, O Christian, the significance of Jesus' Passion and the Noahic narrative as they are presented in Luther's Flood Prayer. After summarizing God's wrath and mercy in the narrative of Noah, Luther teaches us to pray that "through this saving flood [of Holy Baptism] all sin…which has been inherited from Adam…would be drowned and die." Yes, as surely as the unbelievers died in the Great Flood, so your sins were drowned and killed in Holy Baptism. Bach's music paints a "musical flood," with the solo stringed instrument (the viola de gamba in most recordings) and tenor melodies rising and falling like waves. The instrumental lines move up and down in an arch shape, so that the shape of the rainbow appears visually on the score, a sign of God's covenant of life with you.

And there's more in Luther's Flood Prayer. Here the pastor prays that the baptized would "be kept safe and secure in the holy ark of the Christian Church" and "with all believers in [God's] promise…be declared worthy of eternal life" (*LSB* p. 269).

> *What Thou, my Lord, hast suffered*
> *Was all for sinners' gain;*
> *Mine, mine was the transgressions*
> *But Thine the deadly pain.*
> *Lo, here I fall, my Savior!*
> *'Tis I deserve Thy place;*
> *Look on me with Thy favor,*
> *And grant to me Thy grace. (LSB 449.2)*
> *Amen.*

Friday of Oculi
The Twenty-First Day of Lent

21. *Evangelist, Crowd, Pilate, Jesus*: And the soldiers twisted together a crown

And the soldiers twisted together a crown of thorns and put it on his head and arrayed him in a purple robe. They came up to him, saying, "Hail, King of the Jews!" and struck him with their hands. Pilate went out again and said to them, "See, I am bringing him out to you that you may know that I find no guilt in him." So Jesus came out, wearing the crown of thorns and the purple robe. Pilate said to them, "Behold the man!" When the chief priests and the officers saw him, they cried out, "Crucify him, crucify him!" Pilate said to them, "Take him yourselves and crucify him, for I find no guilt in him." The Jews answered him, "We have a law, and according to that law he ought to die because he has made himself the Son of God." When Pilate heard this statement, he was even more afraid. He entered his headquarters again and said to Jesus,	Und die Kriegsknechte flochten eine Krone von Dornen und satzten sie auf sein Haupt und legten ihm ein Purpurkleid an und sprachen: Sei gegrüßet, lieber Jüdenkönig! Und gaben ihm Backenstreiche. Da ging Pilatus wieder heraus und sprach zu ihnen: Sehet, ich führe ihn heraus zu euch, daß ihr erkennet, daß ich keine Schuld an ihm finde. Also ging Jesus heraus und trug eine Dornenkrone und Purpurkleid. Und er sprach zu ihnen: Sehet, welch ein Mensch! Da ihn die Hohenpriester und die Diener sahen, schrieen sie und sprachen: Kreuzige, kreuzige! Pilatus sprach zu ihnen: Nehmet ihr ihn hin und kreuziget ihn; denn ich finde keine Schuld an ihm! Die Jüden antworteten ihm: Wir haben ein Gesetz, und nach dem Gesetz soll er sterben; denn er hat sich selbst zu Gottes Sohn gemacht. Da Pilatus das Wort hörete, fürchtet' er sich noch mehr und ging wieder hinein in das Richthaus und spricht zu Jesu:

"Where are you from?" But Jesus gave him no answer. So Pilate said to him, "You will not speak to me? Do you not know that I have authority to crucify you and authority to release you?" Jesus answered him, "You would have no authority over me at all unless it had been given you from above. Therefore he who delivered me over to you has the greater sin." From then on Pilate sought to release him.

Von wannen bist du? Aber Jesus gab ihm keine Antwort. Da sprach Pilatus zu ihm: Redest du nicht mit mir? Weißest du nicht, daß ich Macht habe, dich zu kreuzigen, und Macht habe, dich loszugeben? Jesus antwortete: Du hättest keine Macht über mich, wenn sie dir nicht wäre von oben herab gegeben; darum, der mich dir überantwortet hat, der hat's größ're Sünde. Von dem an trachtete Pilatus, wie er ihn losließe.

Behold the man, now heralded in mockery: "Hail, King of the Jews!" The first-century Jewish historian Philo gives the account of a Passover visit to Alexandria by King Herod Agrippa in 38 A.D., a few years after Jesus' death. The people dressed up a madman named Carabas in royal garments and ridiculed him as their pseudo-king (*The Works of Philo*, Vol. IV). In this movement, you behold Jesus being mocked as a parody king in the spirit of a carnival play gone mad. The descending melodic lines in the woodwinds seem to depict Jesus being treated in derision, a mere toy for those who reject the Light and choose to abide in darkness.

Behold the man, who is soon to be crucified! There is nothing sarcastic about the next crowd chorus: "Crucify him, crucify him!" See how the sinful flesh, including your own sinful inheritance from Adam, is hell-bent on death, revenge, and bloodshed. Listen for the percussion-like buzzing in the opening "Crucify him!" (*Kreuzige!*) in the lower voices and the violins. Combined with long-drawn, syncopated dissonances in the upper voices, they create an unmistakable portrait of tension, unrest, and even criminal intent.

Behold the man, who fulfilled the Law of God! The music of the crowd chorus in this movement, "We have a law," is a fugue. Similar to the canon but more complex in its recurring themes, a fugue (from *fugere*, to chase, as in "fugitive") begins with a theme in one voice, which each subsequent voice is bound (by musical law) to imitate. In this way, the fugue is fitting for the words, "We have a law." The ascending lines in the opening musical figure recall the music of Luther's Ten Commandments hymn, "These are the Holy Ten Commands"—notice that the theme is repeated ten times.

Yes, behold the man! In the words of Scripture, the music of the *St. John Passion*, and in the solemnity of the Lenten discipline: behold the man! His crown was made of thorns. His interrogation was the very definition of justice miscarried. And He grants His authority to your pastor to justly proclaim to you, "I forgive you all your sins."

> *On Your thorn-crowned head and on Your sinless soul*
> *My sin in all its guilt was laid that You might make me whole.*
> *(adapted from LSB 452.4)*
> *Amen.*

Saturday of Oculi
The Twenty-Second Day of Lent

22. Chorale: Through your imprisonment, Son of God

Through your imprisonment, Son of God,	Durch dein Gefängnis, Gottes Sohn,
Must our freedom come.	Muß uns die Freiheit kommen.
Your prison is the throne of grace,	Dein Kerker ist der Gnadenthron,
The refuge of all believers.	Die Freistatt aller Frommen.
If you had not accepted slavery,	Denn gingst du nicht die Knechtschaft ein,
Our slavery would have been eternal.	Müßt unsre Knechtschaft ewig sein.

Scholars who have studied the structure of Bach's masterwork generally agree that this chorale is the heart of his *St. John Passion*. Moreover, the oldest score in Bach's hand contains the entire text of this poem, while all other chorales have only the first line of text.

Building on Pilate's desire to release Jesus (John 19:12), this chorale emphasizes three closely related themes. First, the Son of God suffers imprisonment so that you might have freedom (*Freiheit*). This juxtaposition of true opposites is at the heart of what Lutheran theological parlance calls "the great exchange," that is, the good news that the innocent Son of God willingly traded places with guilty sinners. Jesus came to fulfill the words spoken through the prophet, "The Spirit of the Lord God is upon me, because the Lord has anointed me…to proclaim liberty to the captives, and the opening of the prison to those who are bound" (Isa. 61:1), words which Jesus quoted in His first sermon in Nazareth (Luke 4:18). Under the Law, you are captive to sin, bound for eternal death, and unable to free yourself from the capital punishment that you deserve by your fault, your own fault, your own most grievous fault. But this Jesus, whom Pilate now seeks to release and the Jews seek to crucify, is liberating you from the shackles of sin, freeing you from the prison of eternal death, and proclaiming the year of the Lord's favor to you—a jubilee year of forgiveness, world without end—and to comfort all who mourn (Isa. 61:2), just as He was anointed in His baptism to do for you.

Second, the author of this choral text, Johann Heinrich Postel, turns Jesus' prison into a "throne of grace." This term recalls the mercy seat over the ark of the covenant, the place where God was present for Israel and a reminder of His abiding presence throughout the Old Testament narrative. This place of God's holy presence leads you to ask, "Where do I go to receive the gifts of salvation from my heavenly King?" One is reminded here of Jesus' extensive dialogue with the woman of Samaria (John 4:1–45) and their debate over where God's people are to worship Him. Recall that the Samaritans worshiped on Mount Gerizim in the North in contrast to the Jews, who worshiped in Jerusalem in the south (v. 20). But Jesus told of the hour when "true worshipers will worship the Father in spirit and truth" (v. 23). That is to say, the place for the Divine Service of the New Testament is the flesh and blood of Jesus Christ. The Word made flesh is Himself the new throne of grace, who freely bestows the gifts of the Spirit and the truth of the Gospel wherever two or three are gathered in His name.

Finally, Jesus accepted temporal slavery to save you from eternal slavery to sin and death. The idea of slavery of course echoes the enslavement of God's people in the Old Testament. Recall, for a moment, Jesus' statement to the Jews who had believed in Him: "'If you abide in my word, you are truly my disciples, and you will know the truth, and the truth will set you free.' They answered him, 'We are offspring of Abraham and have never been enslaved to anyone'" (John 8:31–33). See the profound blindness of impenitent hearts of stone! The Jews were born out of slavery in Egypt—with subsequent captivity in Assyria, Babylon—and arguably were politically and financially captive to the Greeks and later Rome as they spoke these words. But Jesus came to set slaves free from spiritual captivity and to make them sons: "The slave does not remain in the house forever; the son remains forever. So if the Son sets you free, you will be free indeed" (vv. 35–36). Jesus, then, accepted temporal slavery before Pilate so that you, otherwise enslaved to sin and death, would be set free and be called God's own child.

The Great "O" Antiphon for December 20th is out of (liturgical) season today, but it captures the essence of your petitions to the Son of God this Lent:

> *O Key of David and scepter of the house of Israel,*
> *You open and no one can close, You close and no one can open:*
> *Come and rescue the prisoners who are in darkness and the shadow of death.*
> *Amen.*

The Week of Laetare

"Rejoice ye with Jerusalem, and be glad with her."

Isaiah 66:10

Monday of Laetare
The Twenty-Third Day of Lent

23. *Evangelist, Crowd, Pilate*: But the Jews cried out

But the Jews cried out, "If you release this man, you are not Caesar's friend. Everyone who makes himself a king opposes Caesar." So when Pilate heard these words, he brought Jesus out and sat down on the judgment seat at a place called The Stone Pavement, and in Hebrew Gabbatha. Now it was the day of Preparation of the Passover. It was about the sixth hour. He said to the Jews, "Behold your King!" They cried out, "Away with him, away with him, crucify him!" Pilate said to them, "Shall I crucify your King?" The chief priests answered, "We have no king but Caesar." So he delivered him over to them to be crucified. So they took Jesus, and he went out, bearing his own cross, to the place called the Place of a Skull, which in Hebrew is called Golgotha.

Die Jüden aber schrieen und sprachen: Lässest du diesen los, so bist du des Kaisers Freund nicht; denn wer sich zum Könige machet, der ist wider den Kaiser. Da Pilatus das Wort hörete, führete er Jesum heraus und satzte sich auf den Richtstuhl, an der Stätte, die da heißet: Hochpflaster, auf Ebräisch aber: Gabbatha. Es war aber der Rüsttag in Ostern um die sechste Stunde, und er spricht zu den Jüden: Sehet, das ist euer König! Sie schrieen aber: Weg, weg mit dem, kreuzige ihn! Spricht Pilatus zu ihnen: Soll ich euren König kreuzigen? Die Hohenpriester antworteten: Wir haben keinen König denn den Kaiser. Da überantwortete er ihn, daß er gekreuziget würde. Sie nahmen aber Jesum und führeten ihn hin. Und er trug sein Kreuz und ging hinaus zur Stätte, die da heißet Schädelstätt, welche heißet auf Ebräisch: Golgatha.

Behold your King, who is derided by the unbelievers, even to death on the cross. As the tensions rise between earthly kingdoms and the kingdom of God, the unbelieving Jews invoke the highest earthly power, much to Pilate's dismay: "If you release this man, you are not Caesar's friend." The title Caesar (*Kaiser*) was their trump card and their tipping point, as depicted in the lively fugue with overlapping voices, syncopated rhythms, and an abrupt ending on *Kaiser*.

Behold the King, now at the Stone Pavement. Pilate's act of sitting on the judgment seat was a symbol of authority, similar to the custom of standing up in our own courts when the judge takes his seat, especially if he is about to hand down the death penalty. The name "Place of a Skull" (Golgotha) also echoes the gravity of the situation and Jesus' pending death as He gradually enters into captivity to win your freedom.

Behold your King at the sixth hour on the day of Preparation for the Passover. There are numerous references to the Passover throughout John's Gospel. We read, for instance, that Jesus cleansed the temple when the "Passover of the Jews was at hand" (John 2:13). Similarly, as Jesus worked His miracles (called "signs" in John's Gospel), there are manifold references to the Passover (cf. 2:23, 4:45, 6:4, 11:55, 12:1, 13:1). John's linguistic "mile markers" point you to Jesus, the great Passover Lamb, who is on His way to the most important Passover of them all, to die as the very Lamb of God. The day of Preparation, the sixth hour, the Passover—these are signs that Jesus is the Lamb of God, who takes away the sin of the world.

Behold the King, who is greeted with shouts of "Away, away with him" and "Crucify him!" Here Bach's ability to transport you into the historical narrative is at its best. The words "Away...away" (*Weg...weg*) convey the impatience and frustration of the chief priests through lively rhythms, crisp consonants, and several voices singing at once. The shout of "Crucify him!" (*Kreuzige!*) is rhythmic, urgent, and full of dissonance. In sum, you encounter in Bach's music the rage of the sinful flesh that loves darkness so much that it will settle for nothing less than crucifying Truth Himself.

Yes, behold your King, O faithful son of the kingdom, who stood before Pilate's seat of judgment to prepare the way for you to approach the seat of mercy. Risen from the dead, He reigns over you, a baptismal member of His kingdom of grace, with the scepter of forgiveness and the crown of righteousness, world without end.

In all time of our tribulation; in all time of our prosperity;
In the hour of death, and in the day of judgment: Help us, good Lord.
Amen.

Tuesday of Laetare
The Twenty-Fourth Day of Lent

24. *Aria (Bass, Chorus)*: Hurry, you tormented souls

Hurry, you tormented souls,	Eilt, ihr angefochtnen Seelen,
Leave your dens of torment.	Geht aus euren Marterhöhlen.
Hurry–where to?–to Golgotha!	Eilt–wohin?–nach Golgatha!
Take the wings of faith,	Nehmet an des Glaubens Flügel,
Fly–where to?–to the hill of the cross;	Flieht–wohin?–zum Kreuzeshügel;
There your salvation flourishes!	Eure Wohlfahrt blüht allda!

The first part of this unique aria-chorus preaches the strength of the Law and the reality of humanity's condition apart from God: "Leave your dens of [spiritual] torment." The German word *Marterhöhlen* (as in, torture chamber) is a vivid depiction of man without God.

Johann Heermann, whose hymn "O Dearest Jesus" is used throughout Bach's choral work, once described Jesus' wounds as the very opposite of a torture chamber. In contrast to isolated man, Heermann said that Christ's wounds are the chamber in which the believer may hide and therefore be saved. Do you see the difference between a torture chamber and a chamber of refuge for the weary?

The second part of this aria (starting at the second "Hurry") is a unique musical combination of aria (literally "melody") and chorus. You probably noticed that the bass soloist has the lion's share of the music, but the chorus interjects from time to time with the question, "Where to?" In this relatively rare combination of aria and chorus, then, the choir asks the questions, which the bass soloist answers. The chorus parts are short and abrupt, as if the fellowship of believers is gathered around the soloist, peppering him with the question, "Where to?" The bass part, in contrast to the chorus, is definitive, declamatory, and perhaps above all is as sure and certain as the atonement itself. The entire movement sounds rather hurried, as if the bass leads the way to Golgotha, while the chorus follows on the wings of faith.

So come out of your torture chamber this Lent, O sinner! Come out of the isolation of being cut off from God, of neglecting repentance, and of letting your life of prayer and worship take second place to your false gods. And where do you go? Of course, you do not literally go to Golgotha. Rather, you go on the "wings of faith" to the preached word of the cross, to hear the good news that Christ rescues you from your torture chamber and hides you safely in His cloven side. And there you are safe in "Jesus, refuge of the weary, blest Redeemer whom [you] love" (*LSB* 423.1).

> *Your cross I place before me;*
> *Its saving pow'r restore me,*
> *Sustain me in the test.*
> *It will, when life is ending,*
> *Be guiding and attending*
> *My way to Your eternal rest. (LSB 453.7)*
> *Amen.*

WEDNESDAY OF LAETARE
The Twenty-Fifth Day of Lent

25. *Evangelist, Crowd, Pilate*: There they crucified him

There they crucified him, and with him two others, one on either side, and Jesus between them. Pilate also wrote an inscription and put it on the cross. It read, "Jesus of Nazareth, the King of the Jews." Many of the Jews read this inscription, for the place where Jesus was crucified was near the city, and it was written in Hebrew, in Latin, and in Greek. So the chief priests of the Jews said to Pilate, "Do not write, 'The King of the Jews,' but rather, 'This man said, I am the King of the Jews.'" Pilate answered, "What I have written, I have written."	Allda kreuzigten sie ihn, und mit ihm zween andere zu beiden Seiten, Jesum aber mitten inne. Pilatus aber schrieb eine Überschrift und satzte sie auf das Kreuz, und war geschrieben: "Jesus von Nazareth, der Jüden König." Diese Überschrift lasen viel Jüden, denn die Stätte war nahe bei der Stadt, da Jesus gekreuziget ist. Und es war geschrieben auf ebräische, griechische und lateinische Sprache. Da sprachen die Hohenpriester der Jüden zu Pilato: Schreibe nicht: der Jüden König, sondern daß er gesaget habe: Ich bin der Jüden König. Pilatus antwortet: Was ich geschrieben habe, das habe ich geschrieben.

Yesterday's aria-chorus told you where to go for your salvation, that is, to the hill of the cross. Today's movement tells you what happened on a hill outside Jerusalem on a Friday afternoon.

What happened on a Good Friday? Jesus was numbered with the transgressors, as the prophets of old foretold. The earliest fathers of the church often remind us that Christ could not redeem what He did not assume. That is to say, He cannot redeem human flesh unless the Word becomes flesh. Bach's music is stark and even jagged, appropriate for the cruelest form of the death penalty in Jesus' day.

Pilate posted the inscription, "Jesus of Nazareth, the King of the Jews." Such inscriptions were common in the ancient world, a stern warning to passers-by not to commit the same crime (alleged blasphemy, in this case) unless they were prepared to suffer the same fate. Here Bach marks the tempo *adagio*, "at rest," suggesting that Jesus has come to "rest" on the cross, fulfilling His place as the great Passover Lamb.

What does this act say about Jesus? Consider the importance of the phrase "of Nazareth." Recall Philip's description of Jesus as "him of whom Moses in the Law and also the prophets wrote, Jesus of Nazareth, the son of Joseph" (John 1:45), and Nathanael's subsequent confession before Philip, "Rabbi, you are the Son of God! You are the King of Israel" (John 1:49). The placard, then, reminds us of the theological fault line between those who interpreted it as a criminal charge and those believe in this Jesus, who was to be called a Nazarene (Matt 2:23), that is, the branch of Jesse's tree.

How did the unbelieving Jews respond? See how insatiable their thirst for Jesus' blood was! It was not enough to deliver an innocent Man to death while they obsessed over ritual cleanliness for the Passover. They had to follow Him to the cross, proofread the placard, and then travel all the way back to Pilate to file a formal complaint: "Do not write, 'The King of the Jews,'" etc. Pilate stood his ground, unwittingly upholding Jesus' true glory as the King was lifted high on the tree.

What about you? What is true of Jesus' placard is also true of your name, "Christian." The name was scornfully given in Antioch from unbelievers (Acts 11:26), and yet, what could be more fitting for the baptized? For you are in Christ's kingdom—scorned by the world but loved by the Father—from Baptism to eternity. Thus you are called "Christian," for you were taken out of Christ.

By your cross and passion;
by your precious death and burial:
help us, good Lord!
Amen.

Thursday of Laetare
The Twenty-Sixth Day of Lent

26. *Chorale*: In the depths of my heart

In the depths of my heart	In meines Herzens Grunde
Your name and cross alone	Dein Nam und Kreuz allein
Shine at every moment,	Funkelt all Zeit und Stunde,
Making me able to rejoice.	Drauf kann ich fröhlich sein.
Let me see the image	Erschein mir in dem Bilde
To console me in my distress	Zu Trost in meiner Not,
Of how you, Lord Christ, so patiently	Wie du, Herr Christ, so milde
Shed your blood in death!	Dich hast geblut' zu Tod.

This chorale is stanza 3 of the hymn "Farewell, I gladly bid thee" by Valerius Herberger (1562–1627). Herberger was a Lutheran pastor in Fraustadt in Posen (now Wschowa in Poland). He ranks alongside Paul Speratus and a handful of other "one-hymn wonders" who left but a single hymn to our Lutheran repertoire. But it is a gem. This hymn was written during the Black Death in 1613 and is said to have been sung at every funeral for the duration of the epidemic:

> Farewell I gladly bid thee,
>   False, evil world, farewell.
> Thy life is vain and sinful,
>   With thee I would not dwell.
> I long to be in heaven,
>   In that untroubled sphere
> Where they will be rewarded
>   Who served their God while here.
>   (*Evangelical Lutheran Hymnary* 535.1)

The stanza chosen for the *St. John Passion* connects especially well to Jesus' placard ("Jesus of Nazareth, the King of the Jews") via the phrase, "name and cross." Herberger might be intentionally echoing Luther's threefold description of death: the image of death itself, the recurrent image of sin, and the inevitable fear of condemnation to hell. This fear was not only a constant image in Medieval theology, but it was also prevalent in artwork—from large wall paintings to Michaelangelo's fresco on the ceiling of the Sistine Chapel to gargoyles perched atop mighty cathedrals to ward off evil spirits.

Luther's writings and Herberger's hymn counter this image of the culture of death with the culture of life. The name and cross were given to you in Holy Baptism when the Pastor made the sign of the cross upon your forehead and upon your heart. There you died to death itself, to the fear of death, and to fear of eternal damnation. This name and cross "shine at every moment," for the light of Christ pierces the darkness (John 1:5) until the end of days. How fitting that these words are sung on the highest notes of this familiar melody, highlighting the good news that the light of Christ pierces the darkness of death.

Especially at the moment of your death, the name, cross, and image of Christ crucified—who for your salvation "shed [His} blood in death"—grant you the comfort of being in Christ and dying in the quiet confidence of Jesus' name, which permeates your entire life.

> *Lord, write my name, I pray Thee,*
> *Now in the Book of Life,*
> *And with all true believers*
> *Take me where joys are rife.*
> *There let me bloom and flourish,*
> *Thy perfect freedom prove,*
> *And tell, as I adore Thee,*
> *How faithful was Thy love.*
> *(Evangelical Lutheran Hymnary 535.5).*
> *Amen.*

Friday of Laetare

The Twenty-Seventh Day of Lent

27. *Evangelist, Crowd, Jesus*: When the soldiers had crucified Jesus

When the soldiers had crucified Jesus, they took his garments and divided them into four parts, one part for each soldier, also his tunic. But the tunic was seamless, woven in one piece from top to bottom, so they said to one another, "Let us not tear it, but cast lots for it to see whose it shall be."
This was to fulfill the Scripture which says, "They divided my garments among them, and for my clothing they cast lots."
So the soldiers did these things, but standing by the cross of Jesus were his mother and his mother's sister, Mary the wife of Clopas, and Mary Magdalene. When Jesus saw his mother and the disciple whom he loved standing nearby, he said to his mother, "Woman, behold, your son!"
Then he said to the disciple, "Behold, your mother!"

Die Kriegsknechte aber, da sie Jesum gekreuziget hatten, nahmen seine Kleider und machten vier Teile, einem jeglichen Kriegesknechte sein Teil, dazu auch den Rock. Der Rock aber war ungenähet, von oben an gewürket durch und durch. Da sprachen sie untereinander: Lasset uns den nicht zerteilen, sondern darum losen, wes er sein soll. Auf daß erfüllet würde die Schrift, die da saget: Sie haben meine Kleider unter sich geteilet und haben über meinen Rock das Los geworfen. Solches taten die Kriegesknechte. Es stund aber bei dem Kreuze Jesu seine Mutter und seiner Mutter Schwester, Maria, Kleophas Weib, und Maria Magdalena. Da nun Jesus seine Mutter sahe und den Jünger dabei stehen, den er lieb hatte, spricht er zu seiner Mutter: Weib, siehe, das ist dein Sohn! Darnach spricht er zu dem Jünger: Siehe, das ist deine Mutter!

The pillaging of Jesus' clothing among the Roman soldiers into four parts gives the composer a wonderful opportunity to paint the scene in musical language. Listen for the first entry of the chorus on the words "Let us not tear it" (*Lasset uns den nicht zerteilen*). The lively and buoyant music is built entirely of sets of four, the main theme being sung in four distinctive sections. The rapidly ascending and descending melodic lines suggest the division of Jesus' garments among the soldiers. Listen carefully in the lower register of the instruments for a rattling *arpeggio*, known as the Alberti Bass, which depicts the rolling of the dice. The composite musical portrait is the longest and one of the most stimulating crowd scenes in the entire musical repertoire.

See how it all happened for you and for your salvation! The soldiers—unknowingly, unwittingly—fulfill the prophecy of Psalm 22:18. Consider this messianic Psalm, which Jesus quotes twice in His Passion, in its context:

> For dogs encompass me; a company of evildoers encircles me;
> they have pierced my hands and feet—
> I can count all my bones—they stare and gloat over me;
> they divide my garments among them, and for my clothing
> they cast lots. (Ps. 22:16–18)

Christ was stripped of His earthly clothing so that you might "receive this white garment to show that you have been clothed with the robe of Christ's righteousness that covers all your sin" (Rite of Holy Baptism, *LSB* p. 271).

In contrast to the final action of the soldiers stand the faithful woman and the Apostle John, who is unique among the Evangelists in recording this scene and placing the faithful at the very foot of the cross. Jesus is alone, except for His mother and the beloved Apostle. And He commends them to one another, so that they are mutually cared for while the Son of God is left to die alone. Jesus' words in the Passion are slow, solemn, and austere, as befits the great agony of the scene.

When you were baptized, the pastor spoke only your given name—" (*first name*), I baptize you"—because your new identity in Christ takes precedence over your surname. As His own child, you join the faithful to worship at the feet of the crucified One and to quietly await His resurrection.

May we all Your loved ones be,
All one holy family,
Loving, since Your love we see:
Hear us, holy Jesus. (LSB 447.9)
Amen.

Saturday of Laetare

The Twenty-Eighth Day of Lent

28. *Chorale*: He thought carefully of everything

He thought carefully of everything	Er nahm alles wohl in acht
In his last hour.	In der letzten Stunde,
He was concerned for his mother,	Seine Mutter noch bedacht,
Chose someone to look after her.	Setzt ihr ein' Vormunde.
O man, act justly,	O Mensch, mache Richtigkeit,
Love God and mankind,	Gott und Menschen liebe,
Then you can die without sorrow	Stirb darauf ohn alles Leid,
And need not grieve!	Und dich nicht betrübe!

This chorale is stanza 20 of the 34-stanza hymn, "Jesus' Suffering, Pain, and Death," by Paulus Stockmann. The original hymn, no doubt intended for devotional use at home, allows the believer to pray and sing through every facet of Jesus' Passion and what it means for our salvation. Building on Jesus' care and provision for His mother, the stanza above specifically invites you to imitate Jesus' love for God and man.

As you think about Jesus' provision for His mother, pause and consider the principal feast of Christ in the church year that often occurs during Lent, the Annunciation of Our Lord. On March 25th, nine months before Christmas Day, the church rejoices that the angel Gabriel announced to the virgin that she would bear the Lord Jesus Christ (Luke 1:26–38), just as it was promised of old through Isaiah (7:10–14). And now, about thirty years after the announcement that she would be the God-bearer, Mary stands at the foot of the cross, her heart breaking with an agony and angst we can only imagine. The Medieval hymn, "The Mother Stood," describes the pain and suffering of the mother of God as she watched His Passion unfold before her tearful eyes:

> The sorrowful mother was standing beside the cross weeping,
>   while the Son was hanging,
> Whose moaning soul, depressed and grieving,
>   the sword has passed through.
> O how sad and stricken was that blessed woman,
>   mother of the Only-begotten one!

Behold the true reason for the announcement from the angel: this Child, conceived by the Spirit and born of Mary, indeed holds the throne of His father David and reigns over the house of Jacob (Luke 1:32–33), but in a way that no earthly reason ever expected. As the hymn puts it, "His chariot is humility, His kingly crown is holiness, His scepter, pity in distress" (*LSB* 340.2).

You are baptized. You are free from eternal death. Now what? What are you free to do? The second half of the chorale stanza preaches the good news that you are free to "love God and mankind" that you may die "without sorrow and need not grieve." Having been nourished by His true body and blood, you hear the pastor pray that God would "strengthen [you]…in faith toward [God] and in fervent love toward one another" (*LSB* p. 201). Free to live in faith toward Him and love for one another, you are prepared to fall asleep in Jesus' name and rest in peace, for you are in Christ, now and forever.

> *Jesus, loving to the end*
> *Her whose heart Your sorrows rend,*
> *And Your dearest human friend:*
> *Hear us, holy Jesus. (LSB 447.7)*
> *Amen.*

The Week of Judica

"Judge me, O God."

Psalm 43:1

Monday of Judica
The Twenty-Ninth Day of Lent

29. Evangelist, Jesus: And from that hour

And from that hour the disciple took her to his own home. After this, Jesus, knowing that all was now finished, said (to fulfill the Scripture), "I thirst." A jar full of sour wine stood there, so they put a sponge full of the sour wine on a hyssop branch and held it to his mouth. When Jesus had received the sour wine, he said, "It is finished!"	Und von Stund an nahm sie der Jünger zu sich. Darnach, als Jesus wusste, daß schon alles vollbracht war, daß die Schrift erfüllet würde, spricht er: Mich dürstet! Da stund ein Gefässe voll Essigs. Sie füllten aber einen Schwamm mit Essig und legten ihn um einen Isopen, und hielten es ihm dar zum Munde. Da nun Jesus den Essig genommen hatte, sprach er: Es ist vollbracht!

After Jesus commended Mary into the care of John, John took her to his own home. John was among the faithful (Acts 1:14) when the disciples replaced Judas with Matthias and became the newly reconstituted Twelve. Mary is probably among the witnesses mentioned by St. Luke (1:2), who shared her recollections with him to help in the composition of the third Gospel. According to church tradition, John went to Ephesus and was finally exiled in Patmos (Rev. 1:9), where he received and recorded the Apocalypse.

But this early history of the New Testament was yet to be revealed as they stood at the foot of the cross on the Day of Preparation. With Mary and John standing by, Jesus spoke His penultimate words: "I thirst." Once again you might recall Psalm 22: "My strength is dried up like a potsherd, and my tongue sticks to my jaws; you lay me in the dust of death" (v. 15).

Jesus does not quote Psalm 22 verbatim in its entirety, but He certainly fulfilled its messianic prophecy. He foreshadowed this fulfillment when He directed the Samaritan woman to the waters of salvation (John 4:10, 14) and in John 7 when He said, "If anyone thirsts, let him come to me and drink. Whoever believes in me, as the Scripture has said, 'Out of his heart will flow rivers of living water'" (vv. 37–38). In short, Jesus thirsts for your salvation. And your spiritual thirst is quenched by Him alone.

The soldiers responded with sour wine, probably mixed with water and herbs. But even more important is the hyssop reed, which they used as a conduit to give the bitter drink to Jesus. Thus was fulfilled Psalm 51: "Purge me with hyssop, and I shall be clean; wash me, and I shall be whiter than snow" (v. 7).

Having drunk the sour wine, He said, "It is finished." Notice the rather lengthy pause between the Evangelist's words "He said" (*sprach er*) and Jesus' words, "It is finished" (*Es ist vollbracht*). Jesus' final words in John's Passion are set to a simple, descending melodic line, which will shape the music of the next movement. It is followed by a short *ritornello* or recurrent instrumental section, inviting you to linger for a few moments at the foot of the cross as you consider what Jesus accomplished for you. The first stanza of the following hymn provides the title for this book and captures the essence of the theology of this movement:

> O perfect life of love!
>   All, all is finished now,
> All that He left His throne above
>   To do for us below. (*LSB* 452.1)

Furthermore, there is an important distinction to consider with the words usually translated "It is finished": The word *fine* in musical markings means that something is done, as if finishing a race. However, the Greek word used in the God-breathed biblical text (*tetelestai*) means that something is accomplished, as if completing a beautiful work of art.

Jesus accomplished your salvation, conquered death once for all, and fulfilled His messianic mission. But He is far from being finished with you. As we will soon discover, the Spirit, water, and blood have work to do.

O my God, my rock and tower,
Grant that in Your death I trust,
Knowing death has lost its power
Since You crushed it in the dust (LSB 421.5).
Amen.

Tuesday of Judica
The Thirtieth Day of Lent

30. *Alto*: It is accomplished!

It is accomplished!	Es ist vollbracht!
What comfort for all suffering souls!	O Trost vor die gekränkten Seelen!
The night of sorrow	Die Trauernacht
Now reaches its final hours.	Läßt nun die letzte Stunde zählen.
The hero from Judah	Der Held aus Juda
Triumphs in his might	Siegt mit Macht
And brings the strife to an end.	Und schließt den Kampf.
It is accomplished!	Es ist vollbracht!

The solo instrument throughout this aria is the viola da gamba, a six-stringed instrument that looks like a large violin but is held upright like a cello. It is used only in this movement in the *St. John Passion*, highlighting its unique musical import. Listen to the opening measures and think of some adjectives you might use to describe the music. Sorrowful? Somber? Anguished? It is as if the whole creation stands in awe of the Creator who gave all. The alto sings nearly identical music on "It is accomplished" to Jesus' words and music in the previous movement, but Bach expands the music into an extended meditation on the triumph of the Lion of Judah.

In a structure and flow that mirrors Luther's *Small Catechism*, the text moves from statement to explanation. Fact: Salvation is accomplished! What does this mean? Behold the great consolation for you, the soul injured by sin and death, for the night of death now counts its last hour! Once again, there is irony as the way of the crucified One turns the ways of the world upside down. Rather than the "final hours" being a countdown to your death, in Christ crucified death has met its match, for Jesus' death is the death of death itself.

You might have been startled by the abrupt transition to the middle section of this aria, "The hero from Judah triumphs in his might," etc.

The poet echoes the messianic prophecy in Genesis 49, "Judah is a lion's cub; from the prey, my son, you have gone up" (v. 9). That is to say, the great descendant from Judah will arise in the last days to vanquish His people. Moreover, "The scepter shall not depart from Judah, nor the ruler's staff from between his feet" (v. 10). The One who endured the cross now wields the sword of the Law and the Gospel. His messianic reign of perfect justice and righteousness shall never end, for the cross ends the fray and brings salvation. So John could write with confidence, "Weep no more; behold, the Lion of the tribe of Judah, the Root of David, has conquered" (Rev. 5:5).

The music of the middle section is a triumphant proclamation of the victory of the cross. Bach employs all of the strings, a 3/4 time signature, a major mode, lively rhythms, and an expansive vocal range with large, fanfare-like leaps. Even the tempo markings are profound: "It is accomplished" is marked *adagio*, "at rest," but the "hero out of Judah" section is marked *vivace*, "to be made alive." The Christ-Lion is at rest, but He will be made alive on the third day. The final section (known as A' or "A Prime") repeats the music of section A ("It is accomplished"), but only a portion of it. The abbreviated repeat is a musical reminder that indeed this movement is finished—and its comforting message is as sure and certain as your salvation, procured by the Lion once slain for your sins and raised from the dead.

Lord, by the stripes which wounded Thee,
From death's dread sting Thy servants free
That we may live and sing to Thee. (LSB 464.5)
Hosanna! Amen.

WEDNESDAY OF JUDICA
The Thirty-First Day of Lent

31. *Evangelist*: And bowing his head

And bowing his head, he gave up his spirit.   Und neiget das Haupt und verschied.

This is the shortest movement in the second half of the *St. John Passion*, but it is theologically laden. Eight beats, eight syllables, and eight pitches—a trinity of the number of the new creation through Holy Baptism (1 Pet. 3:20–21)—combine to proclaim the good news that death has left its sting in your Savior's side.

Matthew and Mark describe Jesus crying out with a loud voice and breathing His last (Matt. 27:50; Mark 15:37). Luke recounts how Jesus commended His spirit to God (Luke 23:46). But John simply relates Jesus bowing His head and giving up His spirit. Bach capitalizes on the brevity of John's account and traces the bowing of Jesus' head with a gentle downward movement in the melodic line. Listen carefully and you will notice that the highest note in the line occurs on the word "head" (*Haupt*), even though His head was bowing in death. Perhaps this a musical hint that Jesus, far from being a victim of unforeseen circumstances, died as the Lamb who willingly bears your sin.

In the history of the reading of the Passion, the account of Jesus' death is often followed by a moment of silence. Consider, O Christian, both the rarity and importance of silence in the world and in the church. It is rare because of the noisy world in which we all live, saturated with background music so ubiquitous that we hardly even notice it. Some churches even fill the void by piping music into their parking lots and using "mood music" in their services.

How different it is when we observe a moment of silence in the liturgy to consider the strength of the Law and the consolation of the Gospel. During the confession of sins, you take a moment to reflect on God's

Word and see how you have broken God's Law and deserved His eternal condemnation. At other times we pause to meditate on the Gospel, such as after Scripture readings in the evening services. Silence clears away all distractions and lets you focus on matters eternal. And what could be more eternal than the Creator bowing in His head in death for you, His own creation?

Through the centuries, our hymn writers have unfolded the mystery of the death of God in profound theological terms. Johann von Rist (1607–1667) is one of many Lutheran pastors and poets whose theology was shaped during the Thirty Years' War. Consider the fourth stanza of his Good Friday hymn, "O Darkest Woe":

> O Ground of faith,
> Laid low in death!
>   Sweet lips, now silent sleeping:
> Surely all that live must mourn
>   Here with bitter weeping. (*TLH* 167.5)

Yes, the sweet lips that thirsted for your salvation are sleeping silently, only to arise on the third day and speak to His Apostles and eventually to you, "Peace be unto you."

> *Savior, let Your agony*
> *Ever help and comfort me;*
> *When I die be my protection,*
> *Light and life and resurrection. (LSB 421.5)*
> *Amen.*

Thursday of Judica
The Thirty-Second Day of Lent

32. *Aria (Bass, Chorus)*: My beloved Savior

[Bass:] My beloved Savior, let me ask you,
    [Chorus:] *Jesus, you were dead,*
Since you have now been nailed to the cross
And you yourself have said,
"It is accomplished,"
    And now live forever,
Have I been set free from death?
    In my final agony of death
    May I turn nowhere else
Through your pain and death can I
Inherit the kingdom of heaven?
Is this the redemption of the whole world?
    But to you, who have redeemed me,
    O my dear Lord!
You can indeed not speak for anguish;
    Give me only what you have won,
But you bow your head
And silently say: yes.
    For more I could not wish!

Mein teurer Heiland, laß dich fragen,
    Jesu, der du warest tot,
Da du nunmehr ans Kreuz geschlagen
Und selbst gesagt:
Es ist vollbracht,
    Lebest nun ohn Ende,
Bin ich vom Sterben frei gemacht?
    In der letzten Todesnot
    Nirgend mich hinwende
Kann ich durch deine Pein und Sterben
Das Himmelreich ererben?
Ist aller Welt Erlösung da?
    Als zu dir, der mich versühnt,
    O du lieber Herre!
Du kannst vor Schmerzen zwar nichts sagen;
    Gib mir nur, was du verdient,
Doch neigest du das Haupt
Und sprichst stillschweigend: ja.
    Mehr ich nicht begehre!

This unique movement is a dialogue between the bass soloist (the individual believer) and the choir (the Christian church). The bass melody features large intervals in an expansive range, as if the melody is questioning whether to rise or to fall, as befits the questions in the text, along with ornamentation that sounds like raising the voice at the end of a question. The choir answers his questions—subtle yet steady, dynamically soft yet textually certain—in terms of Jesus' death and resurrection.

Question: Have I been set free from death?
Answer: Yes! Jesus, crucified yet risen from the dead, has done it all for you. In contrast to the unbelieving Jews, who denied the reality of captivity (John 8:33) and remained slaves to sin and eternal death, you are free from death. As Jesus says, "If the Son sets you free, you will be free indeed" (John 8:36)—free to glorify God and free to live in service to your neighbor.

Question: Through your pain and death, can I inherit the kingdom of heaven?
Answer: Indeed! You will never read in an obituary that John Doe died the death of Jane Doe. It is unthinkable, for man that is born of a woman must die his own death. But Jesus died a borrowed death—yes, your death—as the all-atoning sacrifice for your sins. When someone dies, an inheritance usually follows. But this one is unlike any other: you receive all the gifts of salvation and need not mourn the death of the One who left these gifts for you, for He is risen, just as He said.

Question: Is this the redemption of the whole world?
Answer: Yes! Jesus died for the sins of the entire world (John 3:16), embraced all mankind in His death, and reconciled the world to Himself (2 Cor. 5:19). Everyone is redeemed! To be sure, many will die in unbelief and never benefit from the gifts procured on the cross, but those who know their Redeemer by faith receive the fruits of redemption: life, salvation, and the resurrection from the dead.

Throughout this movement, the heavenly perspective (the choir) informs the earthly (the bass), giving voice to the hope of the resurrection of Christ and the final resurrection of all flesh.

> *O Jesus blest, my Help and Rest,*
> *With tears I now entreat Thee:*
> *Make me love Thee to the last,*
> *Till in heaven I greet Thee. (TLH 167.7)*
> *Amen.*

Friday of Judica
The Thirty-Third Day of Lent

33. Evangelist: And behold, the curtain of the temple

And behold, the curtain of the temple was torn in two, from top to bottom. And the earth shook, and the rocks were split. The tombs also were opened. And many bodies of the saints who had fallen asleep were raised.	Und siehe da, der Vorhang im Tempel zerriss in zwei Stück von oben an bis unten aus. Und die Erde erbebete, und die Felsen zerrissen, und die Gräber täten sich auf, und stunden auf viel Leiber der Heiligen.

How was the temple in Jerusalem affected when Jesus died? Here the librettist draws upon a text from Matthew's Gospel, perhaps both to flesh out the history of the events of Good Friday and to capitalize on a wonderful opportunity for text painting. We hear that the curtain of the temple, which set apart the most holy place, was "torn in two, from top to bottom," as depicted by a nearly violent musical figure in the strings, which zip quickly from top to bottom. Recall that the High Priest entered behind the curtain but once a year, the Day of Atonement (Lev. 16), to intercede for Israel. The sense of mystery was truly profound.

The rending of the temple veil offers great comfort. You have probably noticed that many Christian churches are built on the pattern of the temple, allowing the faithful to draw closer and closer to God as they approach the most holy place. In the temple, the holy of holies was only approached once a year on the Day of Atonement. But the tearing of the temple veil makes way for God's unveiled presence in the Lord's Supper. So when you receive the Lord's Supper, you freely walk where Aaron and his priestly successors feared to tread: to the holy of holies, where the Lord was most intensely present for His people. At the Communion rail (reminiscent of the Temple curtain), the Holy Lord shares His holy gifts with you, His holy child.

And how does creation itself respond? The earth quaked and the rocks were split apart, as you can hear in the musical quaking of the lower strings. Throughout the Scriptures, earthquakes were signs that God was moving and moving mightily, from revelations in the Old Testament (1 Kings 19:11–12) to Jesus' resurrection (Matt. 28:2) to the signs of the last days (Mark 13:2). Similarly, rocks splitting open recalls an Old Testament revelation. We read in Psalm 78 that the Lord "split rocks in the wilderness and gave them drink abundantly as from the deep. He made streams come out of the rock and caused waters to flow down like rivers" (vv. 15–16). These cosmic signs preach the good news that the Creator has died for His creatures to usher in His new creation (2 Cor. 5:17).

But perhaps most striking is the resurrection of the saints, who came out of their graves on Good Friday, as depicted by the ascending melodic line. St. Matthew then writes that "coming out of the tombs after his resurrection they went into the holy city and appeared to many" (27:53). Can you imagine tidying your house just before Passover, hearing a knock at the door, and then finding a recently deceased believer on your front porch? But that is the nature of the resurrection: your flesh, though bound to die and decay, will rise again in the resurrection of the just. And you will enter the new and greater Jerusalem (Rev. 21:1–2) to feast with Abraham, Isaac, and Jacob, to the end of days.

St. Matthew continues: "When the centurion and those who were with him, keeping watch over Jesus, saw the earthquake and what took place, they were filled with awe and said, 'Truly this was the Son of God!'" (27:54). And so this Lent, you join with the centurion and a few faithful to confess in reverent awe that this Jesus—crucified, dead, and soon to be buried—is the new and greater Aaron, the Lord of Creation, and the very Son of God.

> *O Christ, my heavenly Aaron, You made peace with God by Your*
> *own blood. Grant that I may rest in peace when I await*
> *the final resurrection of this mortal body.*
> Amen

Saturday of Judica
The Thirty-Fourth Day of Lent

34. *Arioso (Tenor)*: My heart, while the whole world

My heart, while the whole world	Mein Herz, in dem die ganze Welt
Suffers as Jesus suffers,	Bei Jesu Leiden gleichfalls leidet,
The sun is clothed in mourning,	Die Sonne sich in Trauer kleidet,
The veil is torn, the rocks split,	Der Vorhang reißt, der Fels zerfällt,
The earth quakes, graves gape open,	Die Erde bebt, die Gräber spalten,
Because they see the Creator grow cold in death.	Weil sie den Schöpfer sehn erkalten.
For your part, what will you do?	Was willst du deines Ortes tun?

This brief movement builds on Matthew's account of signs in creation from yesterday and introduces the next meditation on the penitent heart taking refuge in the pierced heart of God. You can hear at the outset the trembling heart in the strings, with rapidly repeated notes that effectively pierce the melodic line. You will notice some similarity to yesterday's musical text painting, especially in the descending line for the tearing of the temple veil and musical quaking for the earth quaking and the graves splitting open.

As you read the text of this movement, do any Scripture lessons come to mind? Bach's hearers in Leipzig might have recalled the Gospel for the Second Sunday in Advent, the signs of the end times:

> And there will be signs in sun and moon and stars, and on the earth distress of nations in perplexity because of the roaring of the sea and the waves, people fainting with fear and with foreboding of what is coming on the world. For the powers of the heavens will be shaken. And then they will see the Son of Man coming in a cloud with power and great glory. (Luke 21:25–27)

Do you see the parallels between the poetic text above and Jesus' discourse on the end times? You might look at Jesus' death as a miniature apocalypse. In Matthew's account, the Temple veil, rocks, earth, and graves were shaken as the Creator grew cold in death. The poetic text here adds that the sun "is clothed in mourning," as if preparing for the funeral rite of her own Creator. The addition of the sun is probably intended to connect the apocalyptic events of Jesus' death to the end-times events described in all four Gospel accounts, for nothing says the end has come quite like losing the sun.

Thus a line is drawn from Jesus' death to Jesus' second coming, when the old creation will permanently dissolve to make room for the new creation, even as Jesus comes "on the clouds of heaven" (Matt. 26:64). In the new heaven and earth God has promised to lavish not mere things but chiefly Himself on you, who are already made new through Holy Baptism. "Now when these things begin to take place, straighten up and raise your heads, because your redemption is drawing near" (Luke 21:28).

The music ends on a high note, as is fitting for the question, "For your part, what will you do?" In the next meditation you will see how your part is to crush your sinful heart of stone through repentance to make room for a penitent heart of flesh—yet another gift from the merciful heart of God.

Our hope and expectation,
O Jesus, now appear;
Arise, O Sun so longed for,
O'er this benighted sphere. (LSB 515.4)
Amen.

Holy Week

"But be not thou far from me, O Lord."

Psalm 22:19

Monday of Holy Week
The Thirty-Fifth Day of Lent

35. *Aria (Soprano)*: Dissolve, my heart, in floods of tears

Dissolve, my heart, in floods of tears	Zerfließe, mein Herze, in Fluten der Zähren
To honor the Almighty!	Dem Höchsten zu Ehren!
Tell the world and heaven your distress:	Erzähle der Welt und dem Himmel die Not:
Your Jesus is dead!	Dein Jesus ist tot!

As we begin Holy Week and consider what it means for the heart to "dissolve…in floods of tears," a number of Old Testament texts come to mind. You are probably familiar with the penitential Psalms, those which give you the very words for confessing your sins. You likely prayed Psalm 51 on Ash Wednesday with its petition for God to create in you a clean heart and to renew a right spirit in you (Ps. 51:10).

Ezekiel has a clean and crisp metaphor to contrast the sinful heart and the clean heart: "And I will give you a new heart, and a new spirit I will put within you. And I will remove the heart of stone from your flesh and give you a heart of flesh" (Ezek. 36:26). The heart of stone, which you inherited from Adam, is cold, impenitent, and unrepentant. The heart of flesh, which is only available at the foot of the Highest, is alive in Christ.

As for New Testament texts, today is the traditional day to read the entire Passion of our Lord according to St. Matthew. But before you understand the Passion, you need to understand the Beatitudes, especially the words, "Blessed are the poor in spirit, for theirs is the kingdom of heaven" (Matt. 5:3). The Greek could also be translated as "beggars in spirit," for it is only bent low, broken—yes, begging on bended knee—that spiritual beggars enter the kingdom of the crucified.

All of these images—the corrupt heart, the beggar in spirit, the one who ceases to exist—are preparatory for rightly beholding the life-giving cross, on which was hung the salvation of the world. Jesus is dead. And your heart, dissolved in tears of repentance, is safe because the merciful heart of the Father gave His Son to be pierced for you.

Bach scored this movement for minimal forces: soprano solo, solo oboe, solo flute, and continuo (harpsichord and cello in consort). The lean forces create an introspective setting for this appeal to the human heart to "dissolve…in floods of tears." The reduced forces give expression especially to the oboe and flute, which is echoed in the soprano line. Listen carefully to the lower instruments and you can hear the heart beating. The selection of the soprano voice for this aria is also significant because in Baroque musical symbolism the soprano voice symbolized individual prayers of the believer, inviting you to make this text your own prayer. As the hymn puts it: "O sorrow dread! God's Son is dead! But by His expiation of our guilt upon the cross gained for us salvation" (*TLH* 167.2).

> *Grant, I ask You, Almighty God, that I, who often fail through*
> *my own infirmities, may be restored through the Passion*
> *and intercession of Your only-begotten Son.*
> *Amen.*

TUESDAY OF HOLY WEEK
The Thirty-Sixth Day of Lent

36. *Evangelist*: But the Jews, since it was the day of Preparation

But the Jews, since it was the day of Preparation, and so that the bodies would not remain on the cross on the Sabbath (for that Sabbath was a high day), asked Pilate that their legs might be broken and that they might be taken away. So the soldiers came and broke the legs of the first, and of the other who had been crucified with him. But when they came to Jesus and saw that he was already dead, they did not break his legs. But one of the soldiers pierced his side with a spear, and at once there came out blood and water. He who saw it has borne witness—his testimony is true, and he knows that he is telling the truth—that you also may believe. For these things took place that the Scripture might be fulfilled: "Not one of his bones will be broken." And again another Scripture says, "They will look on him whom they have pierced."

Die Jüden aber, dieweil es der Rüsttag war, daß nicht die Leichname am Kreuze blieben den Sabbat über (denn desselbigen Sabbats Tag war sehr groß), baten sie Pilatum, ihre Beine gebrochen und sie abgenommen würden. Da kamen die Kriegsknechte und brachen dem ersten die Beine und dem andern, der mit ihm gekreuziget war. Als sie aber zu Jesu kamen, da sie sahen, daß er schon gestorben war, brachen sie ihm die Beine nicht; sondern der Kriegsknechte einer eröffnete seine Seite mit einem Speer, und alsobald ging Blut und Wasser heraus. Und der das gesehen hat, der hat es bezeuget, und sein Zeugnis ist wahr, und derselbige weiß, daß er die Wahrheit saget, auf daß ihr gläubet. Denn solches ist geschehen, auf daß die Schrift erfüllet würde: Ihr sollet ihm kein Bein zerbrechen. Und abermal spricht eine andere Schrift: Sie werden sehen, in welchen sie gestochen haben.

The Romans had no concern for the Passover or the victims of crucifixion, whose dead bodies were often left on crosses on the Sabbath and beyond, soon to be the victims of wild animals, inclement weather, and ongoing derision. Thus the Jews asked Pilate to expedite their deaths. The request to have the bones broken is marked *forte*, suggesting perhaps the forcefulness of the request and the breaking of the legs. But there was no need to break Jesus' legs in the darkness of Good Friday. Jesus was already dead and had suffered much more than physical torture that day. He suffered the wrath of the Father for the sin of every man as "all forms of human grief and care…pierced that tender heart" (*LSB* 452.3) To determine if He was truly dead, a soldier thrust a spear into His side, highlighted by an upward octave leap on the word "pierced" (*eröffnete*) and a large descending interval to depict the withdrawal of the spear.

Behold the new creation from the riven side of the new Adam! St. John is rewriting the book of Genesis according to its New Testament fulfillment, as you see already at the beginning of His Gospel, "In the beginning was the Word," echoing Genesis 1:1. Eve was created from the side of the first Adam, and all fell into sin through their transgression. But now, the new and greater Adam reverses the curse of the fall, once again by creating something from His side: "No work is left undone of all the Father willed; His toil, His sorrows, one by one, the Scriptures have fulfilled" (*LSB* 452.2).

Yet this is no ordinary bride. Rather, the new Adam creates His heavenly bride through water and blood. The water that flowed from Jesus' side has pooled in baptismal fonts, to wash away your sin and make you radiant white in Christ's own righteousness. The blood that flowed from His side has collected in the Holy Chalice. There the Groom feeds you, His own bride, with the same blood—death-defying and life-giving—that once flowed from His riven side. The Spirit is hard at work through water and blood: "Water, blood, and Spirit crying, by their witness testifying to the One whose death-defying life has come, with life for all" (*LSB* 597.1).

Here two Old Testament texts are fulfilled. First, the bones of the Passover Lamb cannot be broken, for He is the unblemished sacrifice (Exod. 12:46). Second, on the day that the Lord "will pour out on the house of David and the inhabitants of Jerusalem a spirit of grace and pleas for mercy" (Zech. 12:10), they shall look on the crucified Christ, whom they have pierced: "On that day there shall be a fountain opened for the house of David and the inhabitants of Jerusalem, to cleanse them from sin and uncleanness" (Zech. 13:1). In this way you look on the unblemished Lamb this Holy Week to be cleansed from your sin.

In ev'ry time of need,
Before the judgment throne,
Thy work, O Lamb of God, I'll plead,
Thy merits, not mine own. (LSB 452.6)
Amen.

WEDNESDAY OF HOLY WEEK

The Thirty-Seventh Day of Lent

37. *Chorale*: O help us, Christ, Son of God

O help us, Christ, Son of God,	O hilf, Christe, Gottes Sohn,
Through your bitter suffering,	Durch dein bitter Leiden,
So that, always obedient to you,	Daß wir dir stets untertan
We may shun all wrongdoing,	All Untugend meiden,
And thinking of your death and its cause,	Deinen Tod und sein Ursach
We may profit from our reflections,	Fruchtbarlich bedenken,
And in this way, however poor and weak,	Dafür, wiewohl arm und schwach,
Give you an offering of thanks!	Dir Dankopfer schenken!

This chorale stanza by Michael Weisse is an adaptation of "The Wisdom of the Father, the Divine Goodness," a twelfth-century cycle of prayer that acquaints the eight daily prayer hours to the corresponding events in Jesus' Passion. The text above was adapted from the following prayer for the final hour of the day, which serves as a general reflection on Jesus' suffering:

> Therefore these Canonical hours my tongue shall ever
> In Thy praise, O Christ, recite with my heart's endeavor:
> That the Love which for my sake endured such tribulation
> In mine own agony of death may be my salvation.

The chorale text by Michael Weisse prays to the Son of God for help "through [His] bitter suffering," followed by full-strength Law and the full consolation of the Gospel. Under the Law, the chorale admonishes you to "shun all wrongdoing," recalling the petition to "lead us not into temptation" and the need to flee from the devil, the world, and your own sinful flesh.

Especially insightful here is the prayer to fruitfully consider the reason for Jesus' death, i.e., how your sin caused Jesus' death. To be sure, God the

Father sent His Son to die. The Son gladly submitted to the Father's will. Judas betrayed him. Peter denied His Lord. Pilate sentenced Him to death. A Roman detachment of soldiers crucified Jesus. But it was all to make atonement for the sin of Adam, which you inherited from your parents, and which you yourself have added to with every transgression. Yes, your sin killed Jesus.

Under the Gospel, however, this chorale text bids you to "profit from [your] reflections" on Jesus' Passion. As we near the end of our Lenten journey, recall that we have followed Luther's admonition to explore both the history and the fruit of Jesus' Passion. The history of the week that changed the world is intriguing and important in every detail, but even more important are the fruits of your Lenten journey. In encountering the cruciform mystery, you receive life, salvation, and the resurrection from the dead, and "an offering of thanks" to Him.

There are still more fruits to come. Over the next three days in the church year, you will consider His Last Supper, Jesus' Passion in detail, and His three-day rest in the tomb. And on Easter Sunday, you will proclaim the good news that the crucified One is also your light and life and resurrection.

Yet work, O Lord, in me
As Thou for me hast wrought;
And let my love the answer be
To grace Thy love has brought. (LSB 452.7)
Amen.

Maundy Thursday
The Thirty-Eighth Day of Lent

38. *Evangelist*: After these things Joseph of Arimathea

After these things Joseph of Arimathea, who was a disciple of Jesus, but secretly for fear of the Jews, asked Pilate that he might take away the body of Jesus, and Pilate gave him permission. So he came and took away his body. Nicodemus also, who earlier had come to Jesus by night, came bringing a mixture of myrrh and aloes, about a hundred pounds. So they took the body of Jesus and bound it in linen cloths with the spices, as is the burial custom of the Jews. Now in the place where he was crucified there was a garden, and in the garden a new tomb in which no one had yet been laid. So they laid Jesus there because of the Jewish day of Preparation, since the tomb was close at hand.

Darnach bat Pilatum Joseph von Arimathia, der ein Jünger Jesu war (doch heimlich, aus Furcht vor den Jüden), daß er möchte abnehmen den Leichnam Jesu. Und Pilatus erlaubete es. Derowegen kam er und nahm den Leichnam Jesu herab. Es kam aber auch Nikodemus, der vormals bei der Nacht zu Jesu kommen war, und brachte Myrrhen und Aloen untereinander, bei hundert Pfunden. Da nahmen sie den Leichnam Jesu und bunden ihn in leinen Tücher mit Spezereien, wie die Jüden pflegen zu begraben. Es war aber an der Stätte, da er gekreuziget ward, ein Garten, und im Garten ein neu Grab, in welches niemand je geleget war. Daselbst hin legten sie Jesum, um des Rüsttags willen der Jüden, dieweil das Grab nahe war.

Joseph of Arimathea, described as a respected member of the Sanhedrin (Mark 15:43), was a key Jewish leader who petitioned the Roman prefect. John describes him as a disciple "but secretly for fear of the Jews," which Bach depicts by marking this phrase *piano* (quiet), creating a sense of hushed conversation. By contrast, Joseph's boldness in entering Pilate's residence and risking ritual defilement is marked *forte* (strong, full). The removal of Jesus' corpse is accompanied by a descending line extending over an octave as the Son of God is taken to the final step of his humiliation.

Joseph was assisted by Nicodemus, another secret follower of Jesus, now making his second appearance in John's Gospel. This Pharisee and leader of the Jews came to Jesus at night and now returns to express his loyalty and courage as the night looms. The presence of Nicodemus completes the open-ended narrative in John 3, where we are not explicitly told if Nicodemus was born again through repentance and faith. Here, in Jesus' burial, we see that Nicodemus believed in Jesus and received new birth by water and Spirit through Holy Baptism.

Taken together, these two faithful disciples put the finishing touches on a very important aspect of John's Gospel: The story that began in one garden ends in another garden. Recall that Jesus' Passion began in the Garden of Gethsemane. It now ends in another garden as Jesus' body is laid to rest and made ready to rise again on the third day, where Mary will mistake Him for the gardener (John 20:15).

Similarly, the story of your fall into sin and restoration in Christ began in the Garden of Eden, where Adam sinned and you, with all humanity, fell headlong into eternal death. But St. John, you may recall, rewrites the book of Genesis according to its fulfillment in Christ. St. John does not use the word "garden" in Revelation 22, but he includes the key components of the Garden of Eden in New Testament terms: the new tree of life, the river of life, and the fruits of salvation, where "night will be no more…for the Lord God will be [your] light, and [you] will reign forever and ever" (Rev. 22:5).

Tonight, as part of the Maundy Thursday liturgy, you might see the altar in your church stripped bare and then depart the sanctuary in silence, anticipating the solemnity of Good Friday. As you receive the Lord's Supper this evening, consider meditating on this text from St. Thomas Aquinas which unites the past (including Jesus' burial) with the present and the future: "O sacred feast, wherein Christ is received, the memory of His Passion is recalled…and the pledge of future glory is given to us."

O all-atoning Sacrifice, I cling by faith to Thee. (LSB 452.5)
Amen.

Good Friday

The Thirty-Ninth Day of Lent

39. *Chorus*: Rest well, you sacred limbs

Rest well, you sacred limbs,	Ruht wohl, ihr heiligen Gebeine,
I shall weep for you no more;	Die ich nun weiter nicht beweine,
Rest well and bring me also to rest.	Ruht wohl und bringt auch mich zur Ruh!
The grave, which is allotted to you	Das Grab, so euch bestimmet ist
And contains no further suffering,	Und ferner keine Not umschließt,
Opens heaven unto me	Macht mir den Himmel auf
And closes hell.	Und schließt die Hölle zu.

The care given to Jesus' body in preparation for His burial cannot be overstated. The body of Christ, having made atonement for all sin of all men, is carefully and diligently laid to rest. The text of this chorus gives you voice to join with Joseph of Arimathea, Nicodemus, and all the faithful to consider Jesus' three-day rest in the tomb and what it means for you and for your salvation.

Note the threefold use of various forms of the word "rest" (*Ruht/Ruh*). Jesus rested in the tomb, His suffering past and His post-resurrection work yet to come. And as it goes with any period of rest, it is temporary. Jesus has work to do: Apostles to forgive and restore, the Holy Spirit to send in even greater measure, a mother to encounter and reassure, and even some fish to grill. And of course the right hand of His Father awaits, where He ever pleads for you as your own High Priest.

How does this text comfort you? God the Father rested from His work in Genesis 1 and 2 and established the Sabbath Day for hallowing God's name and hearing His Word. Jesus promised rest for the weary: "Come to me, all who labor and are heavy laden, and I will give you rest" (Matt. 11:28). Perhaps St. Augustine put it best when He prayed to God in the opening paragraph of his *Confessions*, "Thou hast formed us for Thyself, and our hearts are restless till they find rest in Thee." Similarly, you receive the Sabbath rest of forgiveness and salvation in the means of grace. You hallow God's Word, hold it sacred, and gladly hear and learn it. And in the moment of death, your body will be laid to rest, knowing that Jesus' rest in the tomb closed the gates of hell and opened heaven to you and to all who believe.

The music is a plaintive lullaby with the stately beat giving the movement a quiet and reflective dignity. The descending melodic line serves as the primary motif, prominent in both the strings and the woodwinds, depicting a time of rest. Perhaps the 3/4 time signature mirrors Jesus' three-day rest in the tomb. Listen carefully to Bach's treatment of the verbal phrase, "Rest well" (*Ruht wohl*), as all four voices musically descend to the depths to depict Jesus' burial. The noun "rest" (*Ruh*) concludes the first part of this chorus with all four voices descending once again to the bottom of their vocal range as they petition a Sabbath rest for the people of God. The removal of woodwinds gives the second section of this chorus (starting at "The grave") a sense of intimacy as the focus shifts from the history of Jesus' rest in the tomb to the fruits of His rest for you.

God the Father, who created your body; God the Son, who redeemed your body with His own blood; and God the Holy Spirit, who sanctified your body through Holy Baptism to be His own temple, will keep your remains to the day of the resurrection of all flesh. And a host of angels reply, "Amen!"

> *O Lord, graciously behold this Your family, for which Your Son*
> *was willing to be betrayed and given into the hands of wicked men*
> *and to suffer death upon the cross.*
> *Amen.*

Holy Saturday

The Fortieth Day of Lent

40. *Chorale*: Ah, Lord, let your dear angels

Ah Lord, let your dear angels	Ach Herr, lass dein lieb Engelein
At my final hour carry my soul	Am letzten End die Seele mein
To Abraham's bosom,	In Abrahams Schoß tragen,
While my body in its narrow chamber	Den Leib in seim Schlafkämmerlein
Gently without pain or torment	Gar sanft ohn eigne Qual und Pein
Rests until the last day.	Ruhn bis am jüngsten Tage.
Wake me then from death,	Alsdenn vom Tod erwecke mich,
So that my eyes see you	Dass meine Augen sehen dich
In all joy, O God's Son,	In aller Freud, O Gottes Sohn,
My Savior and throne of mercy!	Mein Heiland und Genadenthron!
Lord Jesus Christ, hear me,	Herr Jesu Christ, erhöre mich,
I shall praise you eternally!	Ich will dich preisen ewiglich!

As we complete our forty-part journey through the *St. John Passion*, we end with a chorale by the late sixteenth-century hymn writer, Martin Schalling (1532–1608). He was a stalwart confessor of the faith who endured persecution for resisting the influence of Calvinism. This was the case with many hymn writers in the sixteenth and seventeenth centuries, from Martin Luther to Martin Schalling, who treated hymnody not merely as an adornment to Christian worship but as the sung confession of the Christian faith, even in the face of persecution. This text of this movement is the third and final stanza of "Lord, Thee I Love with All My Heart," a hymn which describes the union of the believer with Christ (st. 1), the need for right doctrine and confession (st. 2), and the prayer for a good death (st. 3). If you examine the entire hymn, you will probably be struck by the union of Christ, the Head, with you, His own body.

This concluding chorale describes the shape of your Christian life in terms of death and resurrection, the very pattern that you are marking in the church year this Lent and the coming Easter season. Here you pray that the angels, who ascend and descend between heaven and earth (John 1:51), would bear you home to Abram's bosom, echoing the parable of the rich man and Lazarus (Luke 16:19–31). The language of "narrow chamber" is an especially powerful reminders that Christ *died*; believers *sleep*. And a peaceful sleep is always followed by a resurrection: "Wake me then from death," etc. Especially striking is the phrase "throne of mercy." In the Old Testament, the mercy seat was a physical object, as were the contents of the tabernacle and the temple. But in the New Testament the locale of God's mercy is the flesh and blood of Christ. Now risen, ascended, and glorified, He will hear your prayer to your last breath, for every petition is written in His shed blood.

The chorale is sung by all voices and played by all the instruments, but this is not meant to elicit a standing ovation from Bach's hearers. Rather, this is a corporate statement of faith, which the congregation in Bach's Leipzig might have sung along with the choir and orchestra. The tune and harmony are straightforward, allowing the text to predominate. Musically, the melody seems to hover between heaven and earth, as befits the union of heaven and earth in Christian worship. The dynamic climax is certainly on the plaintive cry, "Lord Jesus Christ!"—words that recall Martin Luther's spontaneous prayer in times of trouble: "Lord! Christ! Help!"

On this Holy Saturday, Christians around the world celebrate Easter Vigil. As you watch and pray for the news that Christ is risen, see the parallels between the life of Christ and your Christian life. Jesus died and rose to new life. And you, though living graveside, will rise again "to everlasting life and a joyful reunion with those [you] love who have died in the faith" (*LSB* p. 281). God grant it!

> *You who have suffered for us, have mercy upon us!*
> *Amen.*

The Resurrection of Our Lord
Easter Day

And I, when I am lifted up from the earth, will draw all people to myself.
(John 12:32)

Our Lenten journey has taken forty musical and liturgical steps, but the broader narrative of Jesus' Passion consists of five sections: the garden (John 18:1–11), before the Chief Priests (John 18:12–27), before Pilate (18:28–19:23), the cross (John 19:24–37), and the tomb (John 19:38–42). On this Easter Sunday, see how each of these five Passion scenes now serves to draw all men to the risen One.

The One who was betrayed in the garden now appears to Mary Magdalene in another garden (John 20:1–18). Imagine the emotions running through the minds of Mary, Peter, and John! Their world had been turned upside down by Jesus' Passion, and now would it be radically changed again? Yes, but in a way that they did not anticipate, "for as yet they did not understand the Scripture, that [Christ] must rise from the dead" (John 20:9). But Mary's testimony, "I have seen the Lord" (John 20:18), will gradually spread like wildfire, even to your hearts and ears this very day.

Christ, who was humiliated in His trial before the high priests, now appears before His disciples in a state of exaltation (John 20:19–31). Behold the gifts that come from above! What is the first word from Jesus—betrayed, denied, and crucified—to the very disciples who cowered in fear? Peace. Peace for Peter, who denied Him. Peace for the other ten disciples, who were uncertain about their future. Yes, the peace that passes all understanding, an Easter gift from the One who still bears the marks of His Passion. And He will equip His Apostles to bring the word of forgiveness across the years to you.

The One who was tried and scourged before Pilate now appears before seven disciples on the Sea of Tiberias (John 21:1–14). This setting recalls the feeding of the 5,000, which occurred on "the other side of the Sea of Galilee, which is the Sea of Tiberias" (John 6:1). Once again Jesus feeds His people in abundance at the Sea of Tiberias. But more important than earthly fish was their realization that the mysterious figure on the shore was the risen Christ. And He sends them forth as fishers of men, who will catch men in the net of the Gospel and grant them to eat sacramentally with Jesus.

Christ, who was crucified after being betrayed three times by Peter, now charges Peter three times to feed His flock (John 21:15–19), which He purchased with His own blood (Acts 20:28). Peter the denier becomes Peter the confessor. Through His work, passed from the first generation of Apostles to a mighty company of preachers around the world, sheep have fed on the green pastures of the true Gospel and stood in the very presence of Christ. Peter once cowered in fear that his association with Jesus might lead to personal harm, but now he is prepared to die by crucifixion and therein to glorify God.

The One who was buried in a borrowed tomb after commending His mother to John's care says John's testimony, rather than the length of his human life, is the enduring legacy of John (John 21:20–25). The confusion over John's supposed immortality has appeared now and then in various sects, but John makes it clear that it's all about the life and message of Jesus. John is merely "bearing witness about these things" (21:24), that is, about the life, death, and resurrection of the Word made flesh. Exalted on high, He continues to draw you to Himself every time the Gospel is preached and the sacraments are given.

You who have risen for us, have mercy upon us.
Amen.

www.ingramcontent.com/pod-product-compliance
Lightning Source LLC
Chambersburg PA
CBHW030528080526
44586CB00011B/363